GRANTA

DEATH

27

Editor: Bill Buford
Commissioning Editor: Lucretia Stewart
Assistant Editor: Tim Adams
Managing Editor: Angus MacKinnon
Assistant to the Editor: Jean Marray
Editorial Assistant: Tania Rice

Publisher/Consultant: Alice Rose George
Associate Publisher: Piers Spence
Financial Manager: Monica McStay
Subscriptions: Gillian Kemp, Imogen Ridler
Advertising and Circulation: Alison Ormerod

Picture Research: Lynda Marshall
Design: Chris Hyde
Executive Editor: Pete de Bolla
US Associate Publisher: Anne Kinard, Granta, 250 West 57th Street, Suite 1316, New York, NY 10107.

Editorial and Subscription Correspondence: Granta, 44a Hobson Street, Cambridge CB1 1NL. Telephone: (0223) 315290.
All manuscripts are welcome but must be accompanied by a stamped, self-addressed envelope or they cannot be returned.

Granta is photoset by Cambridge Photosetting Services, Cambridge, England, and printed by Hazell Watson and Viney Ltd, Aylesbury, Bucks.

Granta is published by Granta Publications Ltd and distributed by Penguin Books Ltd, Harmondsworth, Middlesex, England; Viking Penguin Inc., 40 West 23rd St, New York, New York, USA; Penguin Books Australia Ltd, Ringwood, Victoria, Australia; Penguin Books Canada Ltd, 2801 John Street, Markham, Ontario, Canada L3R 1B4; Penguin Books (NZ) Ltd, 182–90 Wairau Road, Auckland 10, New Zealand. This selection copyright © 1989 by Granta Publications Ltd.

Cover photograph by Alex Webb.

Granta 27, Summer 1989

ISBN 014-01-2357-1

SUPPORTED BY THE
EASTERN
Arts

CONTENTS

Outstanding new fiction from Macmillan

MACMILLAN

JOURNEY THROUGH THE WILDERNESS – *by Moris Farhi*

'Like a modern day NOSTROMO in taking us through a season in the Hell of South America. Very strong stuff' ALAN SILLITOE

August 1989 publication   £11.95

TAKING THE VEIL – *by James Friel*

A Betty Trask award-winning author with his first novel, *Left of North*, now brings us a second novel of uncanny power and originality.

November 1989 publication   £11.95

A LESSER DEPENDENCY – *by Peter Benson*

'Short and pithy and evocative of place . . . A powerful political novel which makes its case all the more forcefully for being so restrained' JUDY COOKE, THE GUARDIAN

Now available   £11.95

THE LIE OF THE LAND – *by Haydn Middleton*

An astonishing novel of the human psyche in crisis – from a wholly original voice.

June 1989 publication   £11.95

CENSORED TALES – *by Tony Rothman*

A Russia portrayed in fictions; an author/censor with something to hide and an open door into a store of folklore, literature and everyday events . . .

August 1989 publication   £11.95

BATTLEFIELDS AND PLAYGROUNDS – *by Janos Nyiri*

The magnificent autobiographical novel set in Budapest in World War II.

Now available   £12.95

GRANTA

OBSERVATIONS

A Fight in Bethnal Green
Jeremy Harding

B ranco Pavlovic was wearing a bright blue robe. It flashed under the lights of York Hall in Bethnal Green. The fans were mostly local, mostly male and they greeted the light heavyweight with loud applause. Pavlovic shuffled around on his toes, working his shoulders back and forth under the robe. The cheering thickened, and he kissed his gloves; he had a clean-cut look that seemed devoid of all expression. Under the robe was a long flannel shirt with a hood at the back.

Denys Cronin approached the ring from the other side of the hall. He made no show of his arrival, but the crowd, at once alert to his presence, quickly took against him: he was a Welshman, while Pavlovic was a Bedford boy with a solid following in the East End. Cronin had on a pair of red shorts—no robe, no shirt—he looked solitary and business-like. He stood in his corner, jabbing at the air. He was compact, shorter than Pavlovic and fifteen pounds lighter.

Pavlovic had shed the robe. Both men, bleached by the lights, had an unlikely pallor. The MC announced a five-pound reward for a lost set of keys. The crowd was impatient. Cronin tried to loosen up his shoulders with brisk circular movements.

T hey touched gloves and stepped back. At the bell Cronin came forward, landing a big left, straight and solid, to Pavlovic's head. Within moments the two fighters were exchanging hard, furious blows: it was not a fight that could last long. There was no sizing up, no graceful footwork, none of the rhetoric of the game: this was unmitigated invective.

Pavlovic had an elemental stance; he spread his feet wide and kept his head still. He had a way of extending his forearms, clenching his knuckles so that the gloves seemed perfectly spherical. Bright and large and full of menace. There was no defensive aspect to his hands; they were all fist.

Each boxer threw a left. Pavlovic bent low and drove his perfectly spherical glove up into Cronin's head. A volley of punches followed. Both men landed hard blows, but Pavlovic established his advantage—he had the reach and the weight—with two rapid, curving punches from both hands. Cronin seemed to slow up with pain. Another one of Pavlovic's long, adamant lefts sent Cronin's head juddering back. The fighters clinched, and, after they separated, Pavlovic came in jabbing and struck a hard, straight left to Cronin's face. The Welshman blotted up the force of the punch, rocked slightly as the shock spread through him, and fended off another.

Pavlovic looked comfortable, at home in that clean, ambitious body. He crouched and threw the deadly upward punch again. It missed. His body rose from the canvas and hung absurdly beneath his outstretched arm. It was a critical failure. The two men fought their way to the side of the ring. But as Pavlovic stepped neatly to the left, Cronin caught him with a looping punch on the edge of his jaw. There was no real weight in the blow, but it seemed to narrow the bigger man's options, pressing him towards the ropes and driving back the prospect of immediate victory.

Pavlovic must have tried a jab: for a moment the referee blocked my view. When he moved again, I could see Cronin's back and his right arm gliding over Pavlovic's gloves. The spherical, confident gloves. Pavlovic's head had snapped backwards with a speed that seemed to separate it from the sickened expression on his face. For a moment there were two Pavlovics, and then he was all of a piece, collapsing.

He pulled out of his descent, but Cronin drove on with his left hand, pumping until the bigger man crumbled into his arms.

The bell sounded. Pavlovic made his way to the blue corner and crashed down on to the stool. It broke the trajectory of his lifeless form, but the real weight of his body seemed to plummet through it. He could not survive a second round.

The fans had been on their feet through most of the first round and were still shouting as a girl in a bathing-suit walked around the ring with the round card held in the air. Two. When the bell rang, the fight began again with a wild swing from each boxer. Then Cronin threw a peremptory left that put Pavlovic off balance. Cronin followed with more swift punches; Pavlovic was adrift on the ropes. Two more blows and the gum-shield slid from his mouth. He began to roll backwards, slapping Cronin bravely as he went. Cronin came forward, his nose and mouth flaring like a single piece of machinery sucking in air. Cronin backed Pavlovic on to the ropes and struck him thoughtfully with his left hand, measuring him in all his helplessness for a fraction of a second: Cronin then delivered a terrible blow with his right. Pavlovic's head turned violently— perhaps a full ninety degrees—and he was out. On his way to the canvas, he took one more impossible punch, this time a left.

On the count of six, Pavlovic almost rose, almost stood; the count finished; he crouched, staggered a few paces and collapsed, flat out on the canvas. A doctor appeared, and the crowd was infected by a deferential hush, beginning in the corner nearest the body and spreading through the hall. One or two of the men made for the bar; others sat like church-goers, silent. Most were still on tiptoe, craning through the smoke-filled air for a view of the ring, for a view of the body. Some people made for the exit. Pavlovic was motionless.

Perhaps it was his wife, maybe it was his sister—in any case another Pavlovic from Bedford. She was at the ringside, but you couldn't see her for the knot of officials clustered around the body. She let out a loud, demoralized cry, a terrible, high-pitched cry that cut through the officials' efficient concern and *skewered* up into the auditorium. She ran out of breath, paused and began again. Another woman came forward to comfort her, but she was inconsolable. The cry had become an admonishing wail—an assault on the darkness engulfing the boxer, relentless, piercing. Now and then, when the doctor moved, you could see Pavlovic's white torso stretched on the canvas, unequivocally still, the two red gloves like ceremonial objects, and just behind him, the woman wailing. As her voice rose, the murmuring in the hall rose with it, but nothing could keep that voice at bay, nothing would stop it.

SUMMER READING FROM FABER

MOON PALACE
Paul Auster

'In *Moon Palace* there are the hallmarks of all of Auster's writing – the entrancing power of his imagination and his unique ability to convey, coolly and meticulously, extremes of feeling – loss, need, hope, despair. *Moon Palace* is an extraordinary, brilliant book.' *Sunday Times*
£11.99

THE REMAINS OF THE DAY
Kazuo Ishiguro

Described by the *Financial Times* as 'one of the masters of contemporary English writing', Kazuo Ishiguro evokes a highly personalized, almost surreal vision of England in *The Remains of the Day*, a love story which tells of an unfulfilled love and thwarted idealism.
£10.99

TWO WOMEN OF LONDON
Emma Tennant

In this strikingly modern reworking of the Jekyll and Hyde story Emma Tennant has written a crime-story for our times. Underneath a compelling mystery she describes the frighteningly schizoid results for women living in a society which demands of them and denies them too much.
£10.99

REAL PRESENCES
Is There Anything in What We Say?
George Steiner

George Steiner, one of this century's most exciting and dramatic thinkers, examines the assertion of 'the death of God' in a powerfully written book which is destined to become an intellectual landmark of our time.
£12.99

THE PLEASURES OF PEACE
Art and Imagination in Post-War Britain
Bryan Appleyard

Prize winning arts writer Bryan Appleyard's absorbing book *The Pleasures of Peace* is a wide-ranging, accessible survey of all the major developments in British writing, art, cinema and thought since 1945.
£12.99

faber and faber

JOHN GREGORY
DUNNE
GLITCHES

Anton Siodmak played tennis for a living. He was not on the circuit and he was not exactly a hustler, but his ability on the court made him welcome at the better weekend tennis parties and gave him permanent access to the more elaborate north/south courts in Beverly Hills and Bel Air and Holmby Hills and Trousdale and Malibu. He charmed the men and occasionally slept, especially when he was younger, with the wives of inattentive husbands. There were even husbands, it was said, who implicitly encouraged this attention, because their tastes had become more catholic as the attractions of home and family had begun to pale.

Besides his lob—a stroke perfected as he edged past sixty and one that maddened younger, stronger but less talented players—Anton's most negotiable asset was his smile. He supplemented his income from the court, and the occasional bon-bon from those bored and grateful wives, as a greeter in one or two of the more fashionable restaurants frequented by Hollywood royalty. He could be found just inside the door where he would plant a kiss on both cheeks, in the European style, and laugh and exchange gossip and re-arrange his date book for the following weekend—singles here, doubles there and the private screening on Sunday night, Marty's rough cut with a wild music track because Bernie Herrmann's score isn't ready, drinks at seven, dinner seven-thirty, we'll run the picture at eight, Costa's coming by if his plane gets in on time, and Sydney and Claire, and next Sunday, you cocksucker, it won't be love, love, I'll take two games . . .

I did not know Anton all that well—I once made a stab at tennis but was glad to give it up when I broke my elbow—but I would see him at the odd screening and when I ate at the restaurant he would kiss me on both cheeks and call me 'Zhannee' and say that the dailies on so-and-so's picture were so lousy that the crew had stopped wearing the T-shirts with the film's title printed on them.

When I learned that Anton had been killed in a water-skiing accident in Portugal, where he went every summer to play tennis, I felt genuinely sad. He was an essential figure in the local community, because he had the gift of making people feel it was all right occasionally to be frivolous. His memorial service was held, fittingly, on a private tennis-court in Beverly Hills, a vast complex complete with its own bleachers, at the foot of a mogul's estate, a court to which Anton had a key and where he could give lessons or bring the pigeons who thought they could take a set from him. The court was covered that day with Astroturf to protect the playing surface, and instead of seats in rows for the mourners there were restaurant tables with bright cloths and a bar and gay waiters from the various restaurants where Anton had kissed the favoured on both cheeks and passed on the latest scandal. It would be a party, we were told, not a wake. Anton would have wanted it that way.

I came directly from a doctor's appointment in Santa Monica and met my wife Joan at the service, and as I sat there under the hot August sun, death was very much on my mind. I thought Anton had actually died under the best possible circumstances for him, a moment of terror as he realized the inevitable outcome of the accident, then an instant later the eternal dark. I did not like to think of him sick or paralysed, his smile and his serve no longer negotiable. The eulogists, all tennis partners or opponents, thought differently. They praised Anton's independence, which they claimed to envy, his ability to march to his own beat, free of all the responsibilities that came under the heading of 'making a living'. What most of the mourners, or celebrants, because this after all was a party, considered the highest praise came from a producer who said that in twenty-five years of friendship, a quarter of a century of foot-faults and let balls, Anton 'never once offered me a script.' This was a code they all understood, implying that most damning breach of the local etiquette, the favour demanded by a retainer: the sub-text was that Anton knew his place.

The service ended and the parking attendant brought my car. As we drove away, my wife said, 'What did the doctor say?'

There had not been an appropriate moment to mention my visit to the doctor in Santa Monica. 'He scared the shit out of me.'

'What did he say?'

'He said I was a candidate for a catastrophic cardio-vascular event.'

Internal Affairs Investigation

Q: True?
A: More or less.
Q: More? Or less.

A: A name changed. A certain dramatic restructuring.

Q: Time collapsed?

A: By about two hours. But all the same day. And I am not sure whether it was that doctor or another doctor who said I was a candidate for a catastrophic cardio-vascular event. I was on my way to Europe. A doctor, maybe this one, maybe another one the next day, asked how long I planned to be gone. I said seven weeks, including a month in New York. He asked where I was going in Europe. I said Germany and Ireland. He said do you speak German. I said no. He said how many good hospitals do you think you can find in the wilds of western Ireland. I said I have a feeling you don't think I should go. He said I think you'd be mad. He said I'm not going to say you're going to have a heart attack. You could live to be eighty without having a heart attack. I wouldn't bet on it, but it's possible. You have a history. Your father died at fifty-two of heart disease, your uncle at fifty. At this point, I think I mentioned George Santayana, you know, those who forget history are condemned to repeat it, but I am not sure. In any event I am sure he would not have known who Santayana was. He was about eight feet tall and blond and very pleased with himself, really thrilled. He had that look like he thought he could fuck every nurse in his office and then go out and do the Santa Monica ten-kilometre run. So whether it was this guy, this cardiologist, or my own internist the next day who said I was a candidate et cetera, I am not sure. It just seemed to fit better here.

Q: That's what you mean by dramatic restructuring?

A: If I did it, yes.

Q: Anything else?

A: When I told my wife he scared the shit out of me, I started to cry.

Q: Anything else?

A: I thought I was going to run into John Sweeney at the service.

Q: Who is John Sweeney?

A: He is the son-of-a-bitch who murdered my niece Dominique.

Q: Could you elaborate?

A: In late October 1982, John Sweeney wrapped his fingers

around the neck of my niece, Dominique Dunne, and strangled her for three and one half minutes, choking the life from her body. He was tried for murder and convicted of voluntary manslaughter; he was sentenced to six and a half years in prison. With time off for time served and with good time—one day reduced from his sentence for every day served with no serious breach of penitentiary rules—he was released from the California state prison at Susanville in two and a half years. I did not attend the trial. A murder trial is an ugly spectacle, and if my own daughter had been the victim I would like to think I still would not have attended the proceedings. I have watched too many murder trials, known too many lawyers and too many judges and too many prosecutors to have many illusions about the criminal justice system. Any trial is a ritual complete with its own totems. Calumny is the language spoken, the lie accepted, the half-truth chiselled on stone. In the real world, most prosecutors crave to be in private practice, where they would defend the same people whose crimes they claim, as prosecutors, debase society, offering the same extenuating circumstances that are the object of their prosecutorial scorn. Before the first preliminary hearing, I could predict that the counsel for the accused would present the standard defence strategy in cases of this sort: the victim, unable to speak for herself, would be put on trial, and presented in effect as a co-conspirator in her own murder. The prosecuting attorney was equally aware that this would be the defence tactic; if he had been defending he would have made the same decision. The greatest offence of which John Sweeney might have been convicted was murder in the second degree, and in California a conviction for murder in the second degree does not carry the death penalty. If John Sweeney was not therefore a candidate for capital punishment, then the state would have me believe that other lives were more valuable than Dominique's. This is an idea I cannot accept. I would have been quite willing myself to do bodily harm to John Sweeney (or perhaps, to be more honest and less bombastic, I think in a moment of rage I might have been willing), and with a certain ambivalence to have the state of California put him to death in the gas chamber at San Quentin. When the state, however, and its servitors decide that one life is more valuable than another, that one murder is more heinous than another, that there are degrees of murder—some murders not even called murders but manslaughter—then capital punishment becomes a matter of bureaucratic whim, an intolerable idea. I would like to believe, none the less, in a justice regnant. I have worked what Edith Wharton called the underside of the social tapestry for most of my professional life. I know that the laws of nature, however aberrant, rule in any penitentiary system. I would like to believe that John Sweeney was buggered in prison—he was young and soft, perfect material for the cell-block punk—and if so, that at least one of the cons who sodomized him—no: fucked him up the ass—had AIDS, and infected him with it. It is an ignoble thought. So be it. I wish him every ill. I hope he dies a death as miserable as the one he inflicted on my niece.

Q: And why did you think that John Sweeney would be at the service?

A: Because he was out of prison and working as a chef in some restaurant in L.A. He knew Anton Siodmak. All those restaurant people know each other. He had worked for a lot of the people who were doing the catering that day. I just thought he might show up. As a matter of fact, one of his former employers called and asked if I were going to the service. I had the sense he was sounding me out so he could let Sweeney know whether I was going or not.

Q: What would you have done?

A: Left. I wouldn't have caused a scene. I was still shaking from what that doctor said. Also it was Anton's day for tribute, and a scene would have laid a heavy trip on his wife. She said the most poignant thing at the service. You had him during the day and in the evening, she said. I had him at night. At night, alone, then I think Anton would really have been interesting. At night he wouldn't have had to smile.

2

It all started the day I received, unsolicited, a letter from my insurance agent. I have had a life insurance policy for over twenty years. I really do not know why. I have always distrusted life insurance as bad luck, a red flag waved in the face of fate. I pay my premiums quarterly and try to ignore the fact that there is only one way anyone is ever going to collect. I am not exactly afraid of dying, although there are moments when I dream of becoming the first to beat the rap. Which was why I opened this letter from my insurance agent—a gentleman I had never met—with a certain reluctance.

To my surprise, the letter said that my insurer, 'in light of the many changes in interest rates and product design' (I especially liked 'product design' as a life insurance concept), proposed to increase the value of my policy by fifty per cent, with no raise in the cost of my annual premium. I have never thought of the insurance industry as a consortium of altruists and knew there had to be some benefit to them in this new product design, but a fifty per cent increase was not to be dismissed lightly. There was nothing I had to do. A paramedic would come to my house, take my blood pressure, ask a few questions, fill out a form, nothing to it.

And so it seemed. The paramedic, a young woman, did make an appointment, did take my blood pressure, did ask the requisite questions: was I taking any medication, had I the usual string of childhood illnesses (measles, chicken-pox), were my bowel movements regular and stool colour consistent (I would rather be asked about venereal symptoms, about whether I ever had the clap or worse, than about my bowels; my childhood stammer returns and I avoid looking at the questioner as I try to guess what's a great stool colour in the earth tones), had I ever had diabetes? As a matter of fact, I had tested as a borderline diabetic several months earlier, but I had gone on a diet and stopped drinking and my glucose levels returned to an acceptable plateau. No problem, said the paramedic. She would pass the results of my examination—it hardly seemed that, just twenty minutes in my library—to the insurer, who would check with my internist.

A month or so later, a second paramedic, also a woman, came to the house to repeat the tests, the first signal that perhaps I did not quite fit within the parameters of the new product design after all. The problem was that earlier glucose test; the possibility, if it existed, of an onset of diabetes could disqualify me from the programme. Would I see my doctor for a complete physical? Of course. A month later I took the physical. You don't have diabetes, my internist said, but it's time for your annual physical anyway, so let's put you on the treadmill and do an exercise ECG, which had not been on the agenda. Twelve minutes on the treadmill, a heavy sweat. Breathing heavily, still hitched to the monitors, I sat on a gurney as my internist read the print-out.

'You have a glitch,' he said after a moment.

What kind of glitch? 'An abnormality,' he said. It was the first of the terrible words with which I would become so familiar. As he tried to explain the significance of the squiggly lines on the ECG print-out, I kept nodding sagely, feigning understanding, even though they were no more intelligible to me than the seismological charts you see on television after an earthquake.

Is it important? I asked, still trying to appear casual. He was already dialling a number on the examining room telephone.

'I want you to see a cardiologist today.'

I did not get the insurance. But if it had not been for the change in the product design of my old policy, I would not have taken that ECG. I prefer not to speculate about what might have happened if I had not taken the ECG.

Right off I was exposed to the Armageddon rhetoric of cardiology. What I had, according to the examining cardiologist, was a 'critical lesion' in my left anterior descending artery, 'a haemodynamically significant lesion,' according to my internist. 'Lesion' is one of those words, like 'biopsy', that one can learn to hate very quickly. Another doctor, with what I can only construe as high cardiological good humour, told me that in the trade the left anterior descending artery was called 'the widow-maker'. I had a number of amiable conversations with my various doctors about the possibility of my dying. It is a subject that tends to concentrate the mind wonderfully. Quickly I fell into the trade lingo, casually referring to that left anterior descending artery as the LAD; it was a way of distancing one's self from the diagnosis, as if I were not the patient under discussion but, because of my familiarity with the arterial chat, a member of the medical team which was going to do its goddamnedest to lengthen those odds, we can't afford to lose this one, he's too important to the nation. No, to the world. I was voluble in singing the praises of my doctors—'They're the best, everyone says so, there's a medical conference in Shanghai, these guys are over there telling those

Chinamen how to do it'—even though I had no empirical evidence that they were any more worthy medically than the pecker checkers who milked me down when I had my army pre-induction physical. Their putative ability simply became an article of faith; it made me feel safe to believe it, and feeling safe was the priority of the moment. I even praised the prints in their office, as if the quality of the artwork purchased by some medical decorator sanctified their professional skills. There was a Jim Dine in one examining room—'I know Jim and Nancy,' I assured a nurse in that room one day, as if to tell her that the Dines were on my case, too, and watching out for me, making the painter's equivalent of a novena; she seemed never to have heard of Jim Dine—and in another examining room a print of Dunster House at Harvard; better Harvard than Chico State, I told myself.

Being a writer, I knew this was good material, and after Anton Siodmak's memorial service I began taking voluminous notes on every medical appointment and on all the wild thoughts that ran through my head, storing them in a file I called 'Cardiac' on my computer. When my doctors used a term I did not understand, I would ask them to explain in detail, a tactic that sometimes made them annoyed, especially when I carefully wrote the answer down on a yellow legal pad, as it seemed to suggest that I was already preparing a malpractice suit. After I got home, I would check out what they said against the *Merck Manual* and the various medical dictionaries we kept in the house. I likened the situation to the time when my house was robbed twice within a period of six months: I got two pieces out of those robberies, and earned far more from them than the burglars did.

What I felt, oddly enough, was a sense of guilt, mixed with shame and embarrassment. It was as if I had been caught cheating or in a public lie. One or more of my coronary arteries seemed to be occluded: it was my fault; I had put them at risk, in harm's way, because of my own bad habits, my failure to pay attention to my genetic history. Life halted. My wife had to go to New York to deliver a lecture, and to Miami to appear on a television show. The doctors had advised against my flying. 'Go with her,' I was advised by a friend with a cardiac history of his own. 'If you stay her alone, you'll start writing your will in your head.'

In effect, I already had. I was not exactly afraid. There was just a sense of constant apprehension, a feeling that I was living on borrowed time, that death was a constant companion. Every muscle spasm, every shortness of breath after the slightest exertion induced an anxiety symptom. I found myself thinking I wanted to live until I was sixty, which was more than a hop, skip and a jump away. There is something about having a '6' as the first digit of your age in your obituary. It is as if you have lived a full life and did not miss the allotted three score and ten by all that much. I began to make small bargains with myself: I just want to see how that Senate Contra aid vote comes out; I just want to wear my new suit from Sill's, it's all paid for, and I haven't worn it; I just want to give that reading at the 92nd Street Y' in October; I just want, I just want. I saw omens everywhere. By accident I erased Susan Sontag's name and address from my computer telephone directory; she had written *Illness and Metaphor*; I was going to die. The next day, by some electronic miracle I did not understand, I was able to retrieve her file: I was going to live. I did not answer my mail; I did not want a letter to arrive after, the specifically unspecified after. I was ever aware of mundane last times: this was the last time I would have dinner at Morton's, the last time I would have a lube job on the Volvo, the last time I would have kung pao shrimp, the last time I would go to Dodger Stadium, the last time I would see a perfect pair of tits. Ah, sex, the last time this, the last time that, the last fucking hard-on.

'Milk it,' I wrote in the 'Cardiac' directory, 'but no excessive melodramatics.'

In medical terms, I was asymptomatic, meaning that until the glitch appeared on my exercise ECG, I had no angina symptoms, which are the early-warning signals for coronary artery disease. My cardiac profile however was not without smudges. I was overweight, my cholesterol was somewhat out of whack, and most importantly I was following in the genetic footprints left by my father and his brother. What appeared to be the narrowing of the left anterior descending artery placed the whole apex of the heart in jeopardy. Without medical intervention, I had an eight per cent chance of a major, as opposed to a massive,

25

heart attack. The chances of surviving a major heart attack were good, I was told, if I reached a hospital within the hour; with a massive heart attack, your survivors could start saying the prayers for the dying immediately.

My doctors recommended that I first have an angiogram, a procedure by which a dye is shot into the coronary arteries that allows the doctors to calibrate the extent of the occlusion. If the angiogram showed that the lesion was as critical as indicated by the ECG, the next recommendation was for a balloon angioplasty—dilating the occluded artery by a balloon inserted into the arterial system. The balloon is inflated at the point of the occlusion and clears away the plaque (the stuff that dentists are always complaining about) causing the blockage. The analogy is inexact, but the effect is like a Roto-Rooter. With balloon angioplasty, the success rate is approximately three in four, meaning that in seventy-five per cent of the procedures, the affected artery remains dilated; if the artery collapses again, then the procedure is repeated a few months later, and if it fails a second time, then the next option is open-heart surgery.

The admitting nurse at St John's Hospital in Santa Monica, where the angiogram was to be given, had that Miss Ratched nurse-knows-best manner. I have often thought that the admitting staff at any hospital is picked solely for its ability to enrage the patients being signed in, that the patient's rising gorge as he is treated like a child while the paperwork is completed is itself a sign of health.

Nurse Ratched asked what I planned to do while I waited for the procedure.

Read, I said.

'You can watch your soaps,' she said.

I said I did not watch the soaps.

'Everyone likes to watch their soaps,' she insisted.

I said I would bring a book.

'There will be no one to watch out for your book when you go down to the cath lab,' she said.

I said I would give the book to my wife.

'Your wife will have to leave the room while you're prepped.'

Then I would give her the book before she left. 'Most people,'

Nurse Ratched said, articulating every syllable deliberately, 'are happy watching their soaps.'

I was beginning to crack. 'They are not my soaps. I do not like the soaps.'

Nurse Ratched smiled. 'Then you will have a new experience.' She seemed to sense the murder that was further occluding my heart and turned to my wife. 'Wives can be little nurses, too,' she said. 'You can help feed him. They're so hard to feed in bed.'

I did not bring a book. I did turn on the TV set. But not to watch the soaps. It was the day Bob Fosse died. On the local news shows, on the network newscasts, on PBS and on *Entertainment Tonight*, every time I switched channels, I saw clips of *All That Jazz*, every clip ending with Roy Scheider singing 'Bye, Bye, Life', as the Fosse surrogate's life oozes away after open-heart surgery. Bye, bye, life. Just the omen I was looking for.

The angiogram indicated that the LAD was ninety per cent occluded. 'Ao valve area calc 1.6 cm^2,' my report read. 'Ao peak-to-peak gradient 27mmHg; LVEF 55% w/mild diffuse hypokinesis; calcific Ao valve w/decr mobil; non-dom RCA normal; L main normal; mid-LAD 80–90% stenosis, 1 cm distal to large D l; dom circ, OM2 1–1.5 cm 90% stenosis at 0.5 cm from origin LV 133/2; Ao 99/66; PA 24/17; PAW 13,10; CO 7.9, CI 3.5.' In translation, it meant I was a catastrophic event waiting to happen. The angioplasty was scheduled for the following Tuesday, five days later.

It was interesting in a scary kind of way. Casual conversation about a catastrophic event tends to point the mind in the direction of codicils to the will and the order of the speakers at the service, the moral decision being whether I have too much residual Catholicism to go the non-denominational route, with the 'Battle Hymn of the Republic' rather than Gounod's *Ave Maria*. I wrote a friend about the procedure:

> This is how they do it. They make an incision in the left groin and from there they insinuate a catheter up the arterial system into the coronary arteries. There is a live monitor on which they can watch what they are doing and another monitor attached to a VCR that tapes what they

just did. They snake that baby up a few centimetres, then they play back what they just did and plot the next move. It's like they are reading a Michelin map of the ticker. When they finally get to the blockage, they inflate the balloon at the end of the catheter, the LAD is dilated, and if everything works the way it's supposed to work, the plaque is dissipated, and floats out through the bloodstream like shit through a goose. Then we hope that the artery stays dilated.

On the day, I was barbered in the groin, giving me at my advanced age my first Mohawk. Then ten milligrammes of Valium, backed up by a Valium IV. The procedure demanded that the patient be sedated but not comatose, as he had to respond to commands and answer questions. I said to the doctor, 'I don't think I've been this stoned since 1968.'

'Few of us have, Mr Dunne,' he said, 'few of us have.' There was background music, via a high-tech stereo system in the cath lab. It was playing a rather dirge-like Bach chorale when I was wheeled in. Then my doctor complained that he hated choral music and demanded some Mozart, so Mozart it was.

There was also a surgical team on stand-by, in case I had a heart attack during the procedure. The surgeon had, the day before, given me the surgical risk factors, throwing in one I had not considered, AIDS from a contaminated sample of the whole blood reserved for transfusion. In my Valium haze, I started thinking about this blood and began babbling to the doctor that the man who checked into the hospital just ahead of me was one James 'Jimmy' Dunn, and I did not want to get his blood type in case of a catastrophic event. The admitting nurse had made that mistake initially—I got his name tag and he got mine, and he had a different blood type. I think the doctor thought I was going bonkers about Jimmy Dunn, but I wasn't. He was wearing one of those charcoal grey utility outfits that drivers of soft-drinks trucks wear, with 'Jimmy' stitched in yellow thread over the left breast pocket. The doctor kept nodding gravely. 'My son goes to Brown,' he said from somewhere west of left field. 'He takes a lot of English courses. He wants to be a writer, too.' The 'too' was the decidedly antic touch.

Ten days after the angioplasty, I took an exercise echo cardiogram. The results, my cardiologist said, were 'spectacular'. A month later, another exercise echo, and again the results were 'spectacular'. The six-month test was equally good: the LAD had remained dilated; I had lost twenty-five pounds; my cholesterol was way down. 'You've bought yourself a new life,' my internist said.

I did not tell him the question it raised: what the fuck do I do with it?

The first thing I did was go to Germany.

Internal Affairs Investigation (Cont'd):

Q: Isn't that a writer's transition? 'In the summer of my nervous breakdown, I went to live in Las Vegas, Clark County, Nevada.' You've used that trick before.

A: All writing is essentially a series of stylistic tricks. That kind of transition is just one of them.

Q: Was the trip as much cause and effect as the transition makes it appear?

A: No. The trip was not really because of the cardiac procedure, although it was a contributing factor. I was terribly depressed afterwards, the way you are depressed after finishing a book. When you are working on a book, your entire life is focused on it for a period of time, then it's over, and the only thing to do is start over again. It's depressing to think about, especially as you get older. You know exactly how long it takes, and if you live out your biblical life-span, you know exactly how many books you have left in you. Writers never retire, so knowing how many books you still might write is not exactly a reassuring thought. I remember years ago going up to Wellfleet to visit Edmund Wilson. It was Thanksgiving weekend, a couple of years before he died. He was in his mid-seventies, but he still needed money the way all writers need it. He said sometimes when he couldn't sleep he would get up in the middle of the night and read old reviews of his earlier books. There he was, perhaps the one great man of letters this country has produced in this century, and he still needed that reassurance, even when it came from his inferiors. It's a tough way to make a buck.

Q: So the depression was like the post-natal depression of finishing a book?

A: More or less. For five weeks, my life had been concentrated, perhaps melodramatically, on whether I was going to live or die. Then it was over. It turned out OK. But it was a fucking anti-climax.

Q: Why do you say 'perhaps melodramatically'?

A: Because of Vince Dooley.

Q: The football coach at the University of Georgia?

A: Yes. He had an angioplasty just about the same time I did. He left practice one day, entered the hospital, had the procedure and the next Saturday, there he was on the sidelines, yelling and screaming and coaching his football team as it beat up on somebody.

3

Six a.m. I was taking the night flight to Frankfurt. Up at dawn as usual and into the park, sweat clothes and a brisk walking pace, three miles in forty-two minutes, pulse rate up, heart pounding. Good for the ticker? It won't hurt, the cardiologist replied. My new New York cardiologist. Not a man to commit himself. He wears pink Brooks Brothers shirts with a hairline stripe and calls me 'Pal'. I call him 'Tim'. For every minute of exercise you do, Tim says, you'll probably live a minute longer. I do some elementary math. Forty-two minutes a day; say forty-five, three-quarters of an hour. Three hundred days a year (365 days less bad weather days, travel days, sick days—not hangover days; hangover days I force myself out at dawn; penance), three-quarters of an hour a day, that's 225 hours a year: that's nine extra days of life per year. In forty years I'll have logged in enough hours to add an extra year. It makes you wonder about exercise, all that sweating and grunting, all those high-tech shoes and pulse meters and expensive exercise sweats, and the Walkman to get you through the boredom, Jim Morrison belting out 'Waiting for the Sun' and other golden oldies that make you feel not quite so past it, so middle fucking aged. Does it make you feel good, Pal? Yes, I say. Then do it. The gospel according to Tim.

Out of the park for some freshly squeezed OJ at a little hole in the wall on Sixth Avenue. The blue Volvo sedan was parked on the east side of Sixth at the corner of Central Park South, by the St Moritz Hotel. It looked as if it had been run through a trash compactor. The roof on the right side, the curb side, was caved in, the windshield smashed and splattered with blood. I thought for a moment that the Volvo had been sideswiped by a truck, but the street side of the car was undamaged, as was the hood. Something had obviously crashed into it from above. I looked towards the roof of the St Moritz.

'A jumper,' said the cop who suddenly materialized at my side. He made a gesture simulating a swan dive. 'Off the roof.' I tried to triangulate the angle of the fall. There were several setbacks on the higher floors of the hotel, and then there was the sidewalk, maybe fifteen feet wide at that point. I would have thought a body would fall straight down, probably catching one of the lower setbacks. He—or she—must have pushed off with enormous strength to make the Volvo. I noticed that the Volvo had New Jersey plates.

The Volvo had been towed away by the time I went to the airport. In the TWA lounge, I found the story buried, no bylines, in the late editions with the Wall Street closings. The victim was Swiss, only twenty-five, a businessman from Zurich. He had jumped from an upper floor of the St Moritz after checking into a room on the sixth floor. He had written suicide notes—plural—in German, which had been translated into English by the officials from the Swiss consulate who were notified of the incident; the contents of the notes were not revealed. He went from his room on the sixth floor to the thirty-third floor, where he jumped. His body was found at four fifty-five a.m. He had removed his glasses and his watch before jumping.

I would like to think I could converse easily with the flight attendants (those who, in simpler times, used to be called stewardesses), but there is something about air travel that conjures up for me priapic fantasies of the most breath-taking permutations, so that always, when I ask the stewardess what her turnaround time is in Frankfurt (and yes, don't mind if I do have another glass, I like Zinfandel, don't you? Oh, you like the cabernets, I like them, too, I'm a real cabernet man), there lurks just behind my crooked smile that real conversation stopper, 'Let's fuck.' This is why now, whenever I travel, I always bring a battery-operated lap-top computer with me, saltpetre for the day-dream of getting it on with 'Hi—I'm Patti' in the first-class can. So: TWA 740, JFK-Frankfurt, had hardly cleared New York air traffic control before I opened my Toshiba 1000 and created the file, 'JUMPER'.

'QUESTIONS', I wrote,

1. Why did he take off his watch and glasses? What kind of watch? Rolex? What kind of glasses? Ralph Lauren?

2. Why more than one suicide note? Who to? He was only twenty-five. Parent & girl/boy-friend? Was he doing anything illegal?

Patti passed the Zinfandel. Crooked smile at the ready, I asked how many full fares in first class. Zip, she said. Everyone's an upgrade. I guess you see a lot of that now, I said. Companies don't send executives first class now, Patti said. They've got so many frequent flyer miles they don't have to. They just upgrade. Heavy nod: I hadn't thought of that. A little more of that Zinfandel. A quick leer: If you don't mind.

Down lights. The in-flight feature was a Steve Martin movie. I opened the lap-top again. I wrote:

WHAT IF THIS WERE THE STORY? The victim was a woman. She was a young call-girl. The man was from out of town, staying at the St Moritz. Someone had given him the girl's number. Or perhaps he took the telephone number from an escort service advertised on that late-night TV public access channel, the one where the naked, bald, fat guy talks with a lot of naked book-keepers with bad teeth and droopy boobs about what makes them hot, Channel Twenty-three. He had called the service, the one doing all the commercials that night, QUALITY MISSES, and the service had picked up on the first ring and arranged to send the girl over. She had arrived at four-thirty a.m. She seemed nice, attractive and was wearing a mink coat. She said her name was Charlie. She said Charlie was short for Charlotte. She said it was all right if he paid her after they were finished. She said for him to go into the bathroom to get ready. She asked if he minded wearing a condom. He said he would prefer it. She said she liked her hotel clients to wear pyjamas because she thought it was comfortable if they undressed from pyjamas. She had bought a night-gown with her. This whole scenario really appealed to him. She opened her bag and laid out a black night-gown on the bed. She said he should brush his teeth and wash his mouth out with Scope and she would be ready when he got out of the bathroom. He saw her remove a fresh packet of Rameses from her bag and place it on the bedside table. Hurry up, she said. She had dropped her mink coat on the chair by the window. There were French doors leading to the small terrace. She opened the curtains leading to the terrace, and then the doors. The night air made the curtains billow. He went into the bathroom. He put on his pyjamas and his bathrobe and his slippers. He rinsed his mouth with Scope and sprayed some Givenchy cologne on his face. He tried not to think of his wife and children. Then he came out of the bathroom.

Curacao? A little Remy? Patti was holding a tray of liqueurs. Kahlua?

A little Kahlua on the rocks might hit the spot. Two. One for me, one for thee.

A dazzling Patti smile. I'm a working girl, that's a no-no.

Say, what's your turnaround time in Frankfurt?

And why do you want to know that?

An insistent call light from Seat 3A. Miss, I need a pillow, that man has two.

Ciao.

She was not there. Her mink coat was still on the chair. The condoms were on the bedside table. Her black night-gown was lying across the bed. Her purse was on the chair. For a moment he thought she might be on the terrace. He said Charlie. But when he went out on the terrace she was not there either. In the distance he heard a siren but did not connect it to her. He felt a sense of unease. He went to the door, opened it, looked down the corridor, but there was no one there. He did not know where she was. Or why she had left the room, leaving her mink coat and her purse behind. He checked the closets. Perhaps she was playing Hide & Go Seek. He went to the open terrace again. It was now getting chilly. He looked down. And then his heart sank. He saw the people gathering below, on Sixth Avenue. He knew immediately what had happened. Did she fall? Did she jump?

Mid-Atlantic. All lights out. Patti was curled up in an empty seat just past the galley. Michelle was on duty. Michelle looked as if she had been working for TWA since Howard Hughes's time. Michelle had mileage. Back to the computer.

He wondered if the police could figure out the room where she had jumped. Or would they claim she was pushed? He could hardly breathe. They would check the trajectory. She could only have jumped from an 05 room, because each 05 room had a terrace, and from the terrace she would have hit the street, where if she had jumped from a room with just a window and no terrace she would have hit the sidewalk. He wondered if he should get dressed and leave and pretend he had not been in the room. But her coat was there, and her night-gown and her purse. And the escort service would know she had been sent to Room 3105 at the St Moritz. How long would it take to identify her? He checked her bag. There were two credit cards, Diners and Amex, both in the name of C. A. Moran. A charge slip from Bloomingdale's for some lingerie, made out to C.A. Moran. My God, he thought, could it be that night-gown? What else? One hundred ninety-two dollars in cash and some silver, a hairbrush, some loose condoms, a diaphragm, basic cosmetics—lipstick, mascara, eyebrow pencil, a charge card for the Lenox Hill Hospital Health Care Center made out to C. A. Moran, some

Kleenex, a handkerchief, a container of spermicidal foam, an address book, a diary. He looked at the last entry in the diary. It was undated, written in a precise hand. The last sentence was, 'My cunt has been my meal-ticket for almost seven years. A woman who makes her living from her cunt is lazy, without self-respect, self-destructive. I am not stupid, but only stupid women live by their cunt. I must take charge. What can I do with the rest of my life? My cunt will not be young for ever . . .'

First light. Landfall below. Probably Ireland. I would be there in a week.

The entry nearly made him ill. He had given the escort service his real name, because he was of course registered in Room 3105, and the drill was that the service called back, as had the girl, and the hotel operator would not have rung him had they just asked for a room. He should have said his name was Kennedy and he was meeting someone in Room 3105 after a business dinner and an evening at Mickey Mantle's down the street. He put the diary back into her purse. He wondered what to do with the night-gown. Where had she kept it? It would not fit into the bag. He picked up her mink coat. Carol & Mary, Honolulu, it said. Who would buy a mink coat in Honolulu? There was an inside pocket attached to the lining. That must be where she put it. He wondered about C. A. Moran when he heard the voices coming down the corridor. He waited for the knock at the door.

Patti: 'This concludes the audio portion of the flight. Please pass your head-sets to the aisle where a flight service attendant will collect them . . .'

QUESTIONS:

1. Why is he staying at the St Moritz? What is his business and how will this incident affect it?

2. Who is C. A. Moran? Where does she come from? Why is she a hooker?

3. Who owns the Volvo that C. A. Moran had smashed into? What is a Volvo with Jersey plates doing parked on Sixth Avenue at five a.m. Something illicit? Perhaps the owner is philandering and now he is caught as well as the man in Room 3105. Is there a registration in the car? If not, do the police check the licence plate and call the party to whom the car is registered? Who is this party and how does this situation affect him? The same sense of suffocating paranoia.

4. Could C. A. Moran have landed on a homeless person, and killed him/her when she jumped? This gets the press on the case.

5. Or interrupted a robbery in process by landing on the person robbing the blue Volvo?

Patti again: 'It has been our pleasure to serve you . . .' Patti then did it in German. Patti had facets I had not imagined. 'Well, you must have some big meeting today the way you worked all night,' Patti said at the exit. 'Good luck.' *Guten tag*, Patti.

Internal Affairs Investigation (Cont'd):

Q: Would a hooker really be wearing a mink coat?

A: The street-walkers do on Sixth Avenue. Mainly because they're working the hotels in the area, so it's up-market. I suppose they get the coats from their pimps. And those girls on the escort service commercials on Channel Twenty-three are always dressed as if they're going to a charity ball.

Q: Do you watch Channel Twenty-three much?

A: They didn't have anything like that in Los Angeles.

Q: That's not an answer.

A: I watch it occasionally.

Q: Don't you think C. A. Moran is sentimental?

A: Yes.

Q: Is that why you didn't do anything with it?

A: No. That can be fixed. It's the situation the man finds himself in that is interesting, the way he is trapped.

Q: So why didn't you do anything with it?

A: Because essentially all it is really is a movie situation. And at that, only the opening of a movie. The first reel.

Q: Will you ever do anything with it?

A: I just did.

4

On the second Sunday in February, seventeen months after the angioplasty, seven months after the trip to Frankfurt, four months after a MUGA bicycle test—nineteen minutes of heavy-duty exercise stress, 'excellent ex capacity', according to the diagnostic report ('A man ten years younger than you without your history doesn't do half that well, Chief,' my cardiologist Tim said)—I went for my morning walk in the park. It was a time of contemplation.

Since it was Sunday, there were no cars in the park and I took a different route, up the steep grade of Cedar Hill on the roadway behind the Metropolitan Museum, knees pumping, sweat pouring. And then the knees would not work, the breath would not come. I rested, hands on my knees, joggers to the left and to the right and in front and behind, just rest here until I catch my breath. Then: Why was I lying on the asphalt? I did not recall going down. Oh, shit, I must have blacked out. Two seconds, four, five—enough time anyway to slide from hands on my knees to stretched out on the road, like a dead-beat drunk or a homeless person lying on a grate in front of Ralph Lauren's on Madison Avenue across the street from my apartment, a source of embarrassment to the joggers who looked away, pretended not to see, this dead-beat with black sweat pants, the word PRINCETON in white and orange stitched on the left leg, going back, going back, going back to Nassau Hall, no longer in control, the ultimate degradation.

'Are you all right?' A Samaritan, not a jogger, with a canvas back-pack book-bag.

'I think so.' The breath was coming back. I was sitting now, brushing gravel from my sweats, hoping the joggers would think I had only taken a nasty fall, the perils of keeping fit. On my feet. The Samaritan said he would call a cab on one of the emergency phones. No: I'll just wait here for a moment, thanks, anyway. Off the road there was what appeared to be a reviewing stand, and I sat there for a few moments, taking in the Museum and the cold blue Sunday sky, taking stock, what to do, what next, I'd really hate to cancel dinner tonight, dinner out with an anchorman and a big-time agent and a sports tsar and a political commentator, I'm breathing normally now, it's OK, A-OK, I won't even tell my wife, nor Tim, especially not Tim, I feel fit as a fiddle now. And fit as a fiddle I walked home. In the distance I saw my wife walking the big, shaggy, pain-in-the-ass Bouvier down another path, his post-prandial mark and dump. And I knew I would tell her: we had not stayed married for twenty-five years by keeping secrets, however unpleasant, from one another.

I called Tim, I told Joan. We went to dinner with the anchorman, the big-time agent, the sports tsar and the political commentator. My mind was elsewhere.

Tim's test the next day replicated the exercise conditions in the park. Another blackout. You've got a problem, Chief, Tim said. Aggressive diagnostics, and I suspect some surgery, Tim said. Replace that valve—the valve that had not even been much of a factor in the earlier disagreeable episode—and as long as they are in there, a bypass, and then you're fit as a fiddle and ready for love.

OK.

'I think I know how to end this thing now,' I said to my wife on the walk home from Tim's. I knew I did not have to spell it out to her.

'Terrific,' she said, the novelist in her taking precedence over the wife who knew her husband too well ever to express the concern she felt, the husband who was so volatile except in times of crisis.

'It's a hell of an ending,' I said.

EUGENE RICHARDS
EMERGENCY ROOM

Eugene Richards

Once I hated hospitals. My wife, Dorothea, spent years in and out of a cancer hospital. She died in a hospital. I came to Denver General Hospital in Colorado the first time because I needed work, any work. A magazine assigned me to report on what goes on in a 'typical' emergency room. So I began to take photographs, though the painful memories came in a continuous stream. There was no protection from them. I saw cuts, burns, broken limbs, heart attacks, and then, what's inside the human body. When a man's chest was cracked, I saw his heart floating in the pool of blood like a drowned puppy.

But now and then someone who surely would have died lived, and there were children who stopped crying and old people who could go back home. There were also peaceful moments when I talked with doctors, nurses and paramedics. I made friends, and my sorrow and fear grew into curiosity. Instead of watching the practice of medicine from a distance I began to move closer. Then closer. There were still whole days when I wanted to run away, but there were others when I was wholly convinced I wanted to be a paramedic or a health aide. I was acquiring a knowledge. When my magazine assignment was up and I had to go home, I knew I wouldn't stay away. My own momentum wouldn't let me.

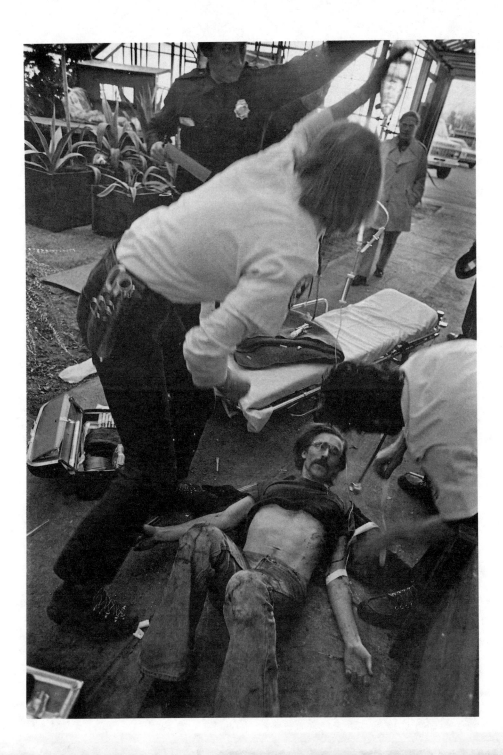

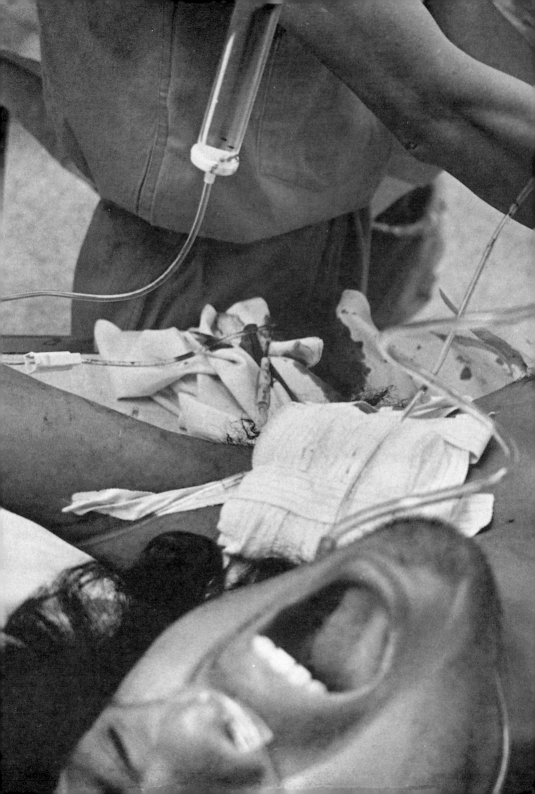

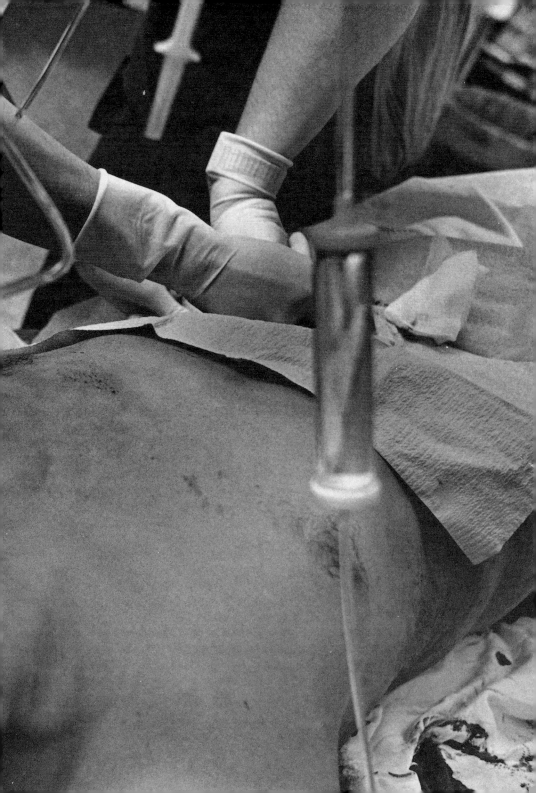

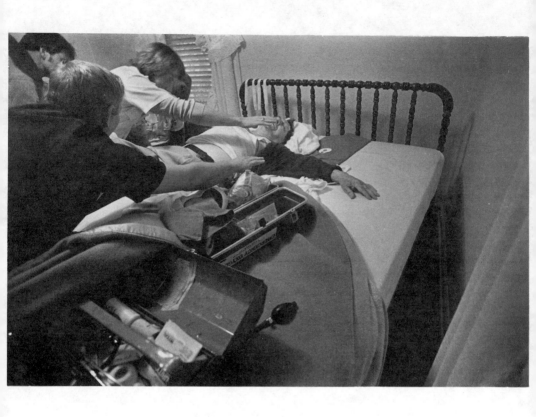

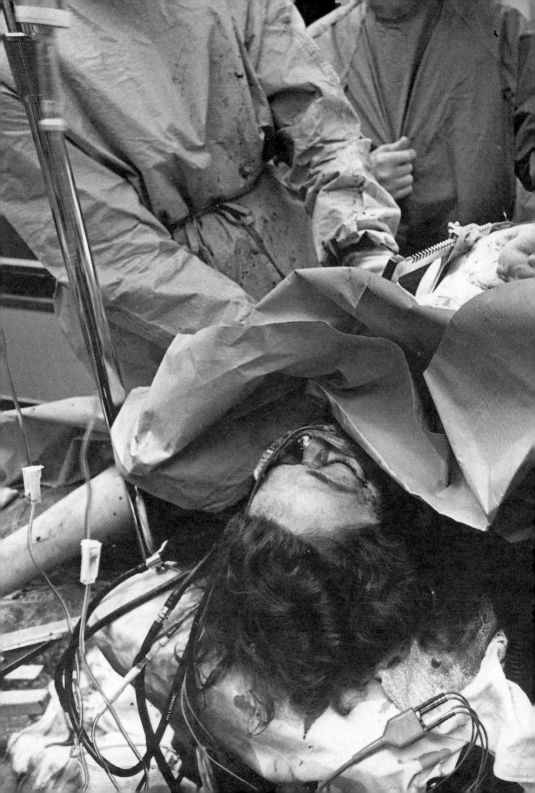

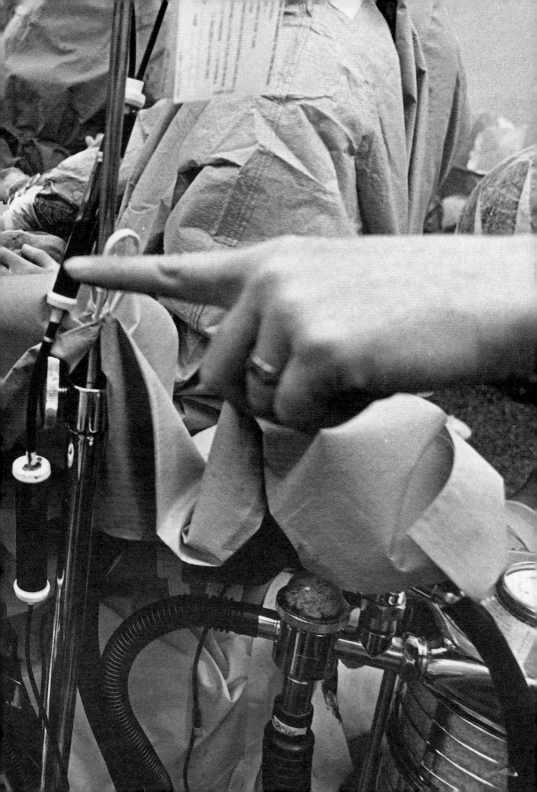

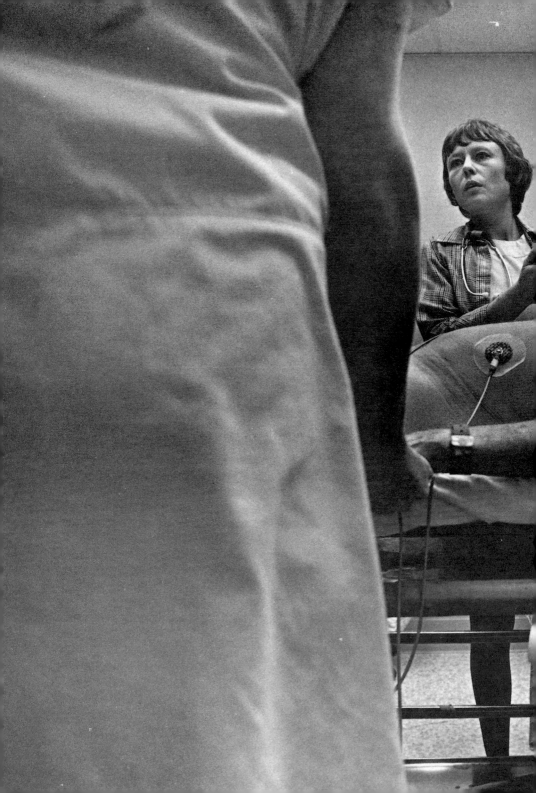

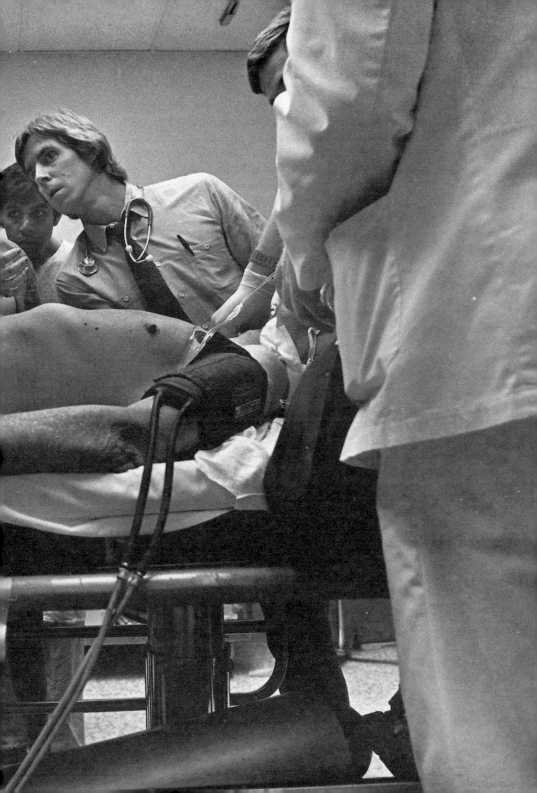

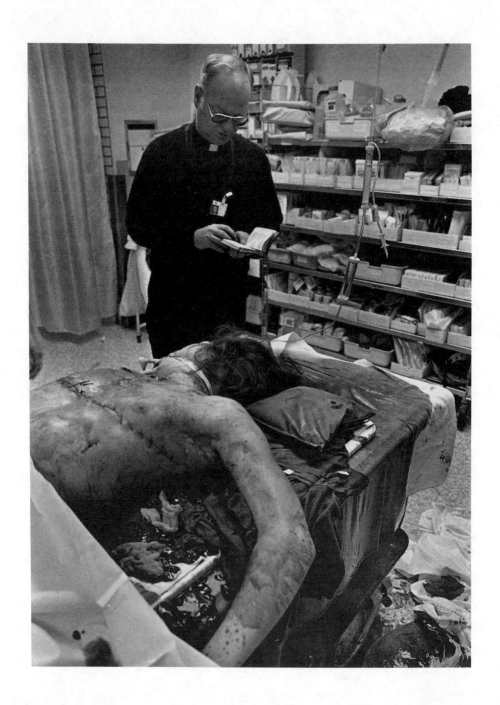

JOHN BERGER

Once in Europa

A farmer sits in a barn at night, playing the accordion to himself. Another feeds a bonfire with the corpses of dozens of dead sheep, his entire flock struck by lightning. A woman watches an old man shouting his name from a hillside into the wind.

Around such images John Berger, in his first fiction for six years, builds pictures of whole lives. The narratives in *Once in Europa* are above all love stories, though the love might be the devotion of a bachelor son to his widowed mother, or the hopeless, humiliating infatuation of a solitary farmer for a woman from the town.

But in tracing the course of love and its consequences, these stories do more: they depict precisely, and utterly without sentimentality, the life of a community uniquely determined by the work it does – the annual raising of livestock, the cultivation of the land – its labour governed and dignified by the seasons and elements.

'Marvellous stories, remarkable for their quality of visionary intimacy.'
Angela Carter in *The New York Times Book Review*

JOHN BERGER, art historian, essayist, poet and novelist, was born in London in 1928. His many books include *The Success and Failure of Picasso* and *G*, the novel for which he won the Booker Prize in 1972.

John Berger now lives and works in a small peasant community in the French Alps. This milieu is the setting for *Pig Earth* and *Once in Europa*, the first two volumes of his trilogy 'Into Their Labours' that evokes, in fictional form, the peasant's odyssey from village to metropolis.

On sale 1 September
from all good bookshops
price £10.95 (hardback)

JOHN BERGER AND JEAN MOHR

A Fortunate Man

John Sassall is a country doctor who has chosen to practise alone in an isolated and depressed English rural community. The people he serves trust him almost without question. He is doing what he wants to do.

In this honest and moving book, John Berger and Jean Mohr show the complex relationship between Sassall, his patients and their environment, and question at what social cost Sassall can consider himself a fortunate man.

Available now from
all good bookshops
price £6.99

JOHN BERGER AND JEAN MOHR

A Seventh Man

Why do the industrial European countries depend on importing twenty-two million hands and arms to do the most menial work? Why are the owners of those arms and hands treated like replaceable parts of a machine? What compels the migrant worker to leave his village and accept this humiliation?

Continuing the collaboration begun in *A Fortunate Man*, John Berger's text and Jean Mohr's photographs are at the same time disturbing and compassionate. *A Seventh Man* shows that the migrant worker, far from being on the margins of modern experience, is absolutely central to it.

Available now from
all good bookshops
price £6.99

JOHN BERGER AND JEAN MOHR

Another Way of Telling

With the invention of photography we acquired a means of expression more closely associated with memory than any other. But exactly how and why do photographs move us? What can we learn from family albums and the private use of photographs? Do appearances constitute a code of life, a sort of 'half-language'?

These are some of the questions examined in *Another Way of Telling*, in which John Berger and Jean Mohr lay the groundwork for a new theory of photography. No book of photographs quite resembles this one, with its mixture of stories, theory, portrait and confession. Its principal tale, told without words in 150 photographs, concerns the life of a fictional peasant woman. It is not cinematic and has nothing to do with reportage. It constitutes another way of telling.

Available now from
all good bookshops
price £7.99

EDMUND WHITE
SKINNED ALIVE

I first saw him at a reading in Paris. An American writer, whom everyone had supposed dead, had come to France to launch a new translation of his classic book, originally published twenty-five years earlier. The young man in the audience who caught my eye had short red-blond hair and broad shoulders (bodyguard broad, commando broad) and an unsmiling gravity. When he spoke English, he was very serious; when he spoke French, he looked amused.

He was seated on the other side of the semi-circle surrounding the author, who was slowly, sweetly, suicidally disappointing the young members of his audience. They had all come expecting to meet Satan, for hadn't he summed up in his pages a brutish vision of gang rape in burned-out lots, of drug betrayals and teen-age murders? But what they faced now was a reformed drunk given to optimism, offering us brief recipes for recovery and serenity—not at all what the spiky-haired audience had had in mind. I was charmed by the writer's hearty laugh and pleased that he'd been able to trade in his large bacchanalian genius for a bit of happiness. But his new writings were painful to listen to and my eyes wandered restlessly over the book shelves. I was searching out interesting new titles, saluting familiar ones, reproaching a few.

And then I had the young man to look at. He had on black trousers full in the calf and narrow in the thighs, his compact waist cinched in by a thick black belt and a gold buckle. His torso was concealed by an extremely ample, long-sleeved black shirt, but despite its fullness I could still see the broad, powerful chest, the massive shoulders and biceps—the body of a professional killer. His neck was thick, like cambered marble.

My French friend Hélène nudged me and whispered, 'There's one for you.' Maybe she said that later, during the discussion period after the young man had asked a question that revealed his complete familiarity with the text. He had a tenor voice he'd worked to lower or perhaps he was just shy—one, in any event, that made me think of those low notes a cellist draws out of his instrument by slowly sawing the bow back and forth while fingering a tremolo with the other hand.

From his accent I couldn't be certain he was American;

Opposite: Edmund White in Taroudannt, Morocco.

he might be German, a nationality that seemed to accommodate his contradictions better—young but dignified, athletic but intellectual. There was nothing about him of the brash American college kid, the joker who has been encouraged to express all his opinions, including those that have just popped into his head. The young man respected the author's classic novel so much that he made me want to take it more seriously. I liked the way he referred to specific scenes as though they were literary sites known to everyone. This grave young man was probably right, the scandalous books always turn out to be the good ones.

Yes, Hélène must have nudged me after his question, because she's attracted to men only if they're intelligent. If they're literary, all the better, since, when she's not reading, she's talking about books. I'll phone her towards noon and she'll say, 'I'm in China,' or, 'Today, it's the Palais Royale,' or, 'Another unhappy American childhood,' depending on whether the book is a guide, a memoir or a novel. She worries about me and wants me to find someone, preferably a Parisian, so I won't get any funny ideas about moving back to New York. She and I always speak in English. If I trick her into continuing in French after an evening with friends, she'll suddenly catch herself and say indignantly, 'But why in earth are we speaking French!' She claims to be bilingual, but she speaks French to her cats. People dream in the language they use on their cats.

She is too discreet, even with me, her closest friend, to solicit any details about my intimate life. Once, when she could sense Jean-Loup was making me unhappy, I said to her, 'But you know I do have two other . . . people I see from time to time,' and she smiled, patted my hand and said, 'Good. Very good. I'm delighted.' Another time she shocked me. I asked her what I should say to a jealous lover, and she replied, 'The answer to the question, "Are you faithful, *chéri*?" is always "Yes."' She made vague efforts to meet and even charm the different men who passed through my life (her Japanese clothes, low voice and blue-tinted glasses impressed them all). But I could tell she disapproved of most of them. 'It's Saturday,' she would say. 'Jean-Loup must be rounding you up for your afternoon shopping spree.' If ever I said anything against him, she would dramatically bite her lip, look me in the eye and nod.

But I liked to please Jean-Loup. And if I bought him his clothes every Saturday, he would let me take them off again, piece by piece, to expose his boyish body, a body as lean-hipped and priapic as those Cretan youths painted on the walls of Minos's palace. On one hip, the colour of wedding-gown satin, he had a mole, which the French more accurately call a *grain de beauté*.

Since Jean-Loup came from a solid middle-class family but had climbed a social rung, he had the most rigid code of etiquette, and I owe him the slight improvements I've made in my impressionistic American table manners, learned thirty years ago among boarding-school savages. Whereas Americans are taught to keep their unused hand in their laps at table, the French are so filthy-minded they assume hidden hands are the devil's workshop. Whereas Americans clear each plate as soon as it's finished, the French wait for everyone to complete their meal. That's the sort of thing he taught me. To light a match after one has smelled up a toilet. To greet the most bizarre story with the comment, 'But that's perfectly normal.' To be careful to serve oneself from the cheese tray no more than once, ('Cheese is the only course a guest has the right to refuse,' he told me, 'and the only dish that should never be passed twice').

Also not to ask so many questions or volunteer so many answers. After a two-hour train ride he'd ask me if I had had enough time to confide to the stranger at my side all the details of my unhappy American childhood. Like most Frenchmen who have affairs with Americans, he was attracted by my 'niceness' and 'simplicity' (ambiguous compliments at best), but had set out to reform those very qualities, which became weaknesses once I was granted the high status of honorary Frenchman. 'Not Frenchman,' he would say. 'You'll never be French. But you are a Parisian. No one can deny that.' Then to flatter me he would add, '*Plus parisien tu meurs*,' though just then I felt I'd die if I were less, not more Parisian.

But if Jean-Loup was always 'correct' in the salon, he was 'vicious' and 'perverse' (high compliments in French) in the boudoir. The problem was that he didn't like to see me very often.

He loved me but wasn't in love with me, that depressing (and all too translatable) distinction ('*Je t'aime mais je ne suis pas amoureux*'). He was always on the train to Bordeaux, where his parents lived and where he'd been admitted to several châteaux, including some familiar even to me because they were on wine labels. He'd come back with stories of weekend country parties at which the boys got drunk and tore off the girls' designer dresses and then everyone went riding bareback at dawn. He had a set of phrases for describing these routs ('*On s'éclatait*;' '*On se démarrait*;' '*On était fou, mais vraiment fou et on a bien rigolé*'), which all meant they had behaved disreputably with the right people within decorous limits. After all they were all in their own 'milieu'. He slept with a few of the girls and was looking to marry one who would be intelligent, not ugly, distinguished, a good sport and a slut in bed. He was all those things, so he was only looking for his counterpart. He even asked me to help him. 'You go everywhere, you meet everyone,' he said, 'you've fixed up so many of your friends, find me someone like Brigitte but better groomed, a good slut who likes men. Of course, even if I married that would never affect our relationship.' Recently he'd decided that he would inform his bride-to-be that he was homosexual; he just knew she'd be worldly about it.

With friends Jean-Loup was jolly and impertinent, quick to trot out his 'horrors', as he called them, things that would make the girls scream and the boys blush. Twice he showed his penis at mixed dinner parties. Even so, his 'horrors' were, while shocking, kind-hearted and astute. He never asked about money or class, questions that might really embarrass a French man. He would sooner ask about blow-jobs than job prospects, cock-size than the size of a raise. In our funny makeshift circle—which I had cobbled together to amuse him and which fell apart when he left me—the girls were witty, uncomplicated and heterosexual, and the boys handsome and homo. We were resolutely silly and made enormous occasions out of each other's birthdays and saint's days. Our serious, intimate conversations took place only between two people, usually over the phone.

I neglected friends my own age. I never spoke English or talked about books except with Hélène. A friend from New York said, after staying with me for a week, that I was living in a fool's paradise, a gilded play-pen filled with enchanting, radiant nymphs and satyrs who offered me 'no challenge'. He disapproved of the way I was willing to take just crumbs from Jean-Loup.

Brioche crumbs, I thought.

I didn't know how to explain that now that so many of my old friends in New York had died—my best friend, and also my editor, a real friend as well—I preferred my play-pen, where I could be twenty-five again but French this time. When reminded of my real age and nationality, I then *played* at being older and American. Youth and age seemed equally theatrical. Maybe the unreality was the effect of living in another language, of worrying about how many slices of *chèvre* one could take and of buying pretty clothes for a bisexual Bordelais. At about this time a punk interviewed me on television and asked, 'You are known as a homosexual, a writer and an American. When did you first realize you were an American?'

'When I moved to France,' I said.

That Jean-Loup was elusive could not be held against him. He warned me from the first he was in full flight. What I didn't grasp was that he was running towards someone even he couldn't name yet. Despite his lucid way of making distinctions about other people ('She's not a liar but a mythomaniac; her lying serves no purpose') he was indecisive about everything in his own future: Would he marry or become completely gay? Would he stay in business or develop his talent, drawing adult comic strips? Would he remain in Paris or continue shuttling between it and Bordeaux? I teased him, calling him, 'Monsieur Charnière' ('Mister Hinge').

Where he could be decisive was in bed. He had precise and highly coloured fantasies, which I deduced from his paces and those he put me through. He never talked about his desires until the last few times we had sex, just before the end of our 'story' as the French call an affair; his new talkativeness I took as a sign that he'd lost interest in me or at least respect for me, and I was right.

Earlier he had never talked about his desire, but hurled it against me: he needed me here not there, like this not that. I felt desired for the first time in years.

My friends, especially Hélène, but even the other children in the play-pen, assumed Jean-Loup was genteelly fleecing me with my worldly, cheerful complicity, but I knew I had too little money to warrant such a speculation. He'd even told me that if it was money he was after he could find a man far richer than me. In fact I knew I excited him. That's why I had to find him a distinguished slut for a wife. I had corrupted him, he told me, by habituating him to sex that was 'hard', which the French pronounce 'ard' as in *ardent* and, out of a certain deference, never elide with the preceding word.

He didn't mind if I talked during sex, telling him who he was, where we were and why I had to do all this to him. I was used to sex raps from the drug-taking 1970s. Now, of course, there were no drugs and I had to find French words for my obsessions, and when I sometimes made a mistake in gender or verb form Jean-Loup would wince. He wouldn't mention it later; he didn't want to talk anything over later. Only once, after he'd done something very strange to me, he asked, laughing as he emerged from the shower, 'Are you the crazy one or am I? I think we're both crazy.' He seemed very pleased.

For the first year we'd struggled to be 'lovers' officially, but he devoted more of his energy to warding me off than embracing me. He had a rule that he could never stay on after a dinner at my place; he would always leave with the other members of the play-pen. To stay behind would look too domestic, he thought, too queer, too *pédé*. After a year of such partial intimacy I got fed up. More likely I became frightened that Jean-Loup, who was growng increasingly remote, would suddenly drop me. I broke up with him over dinner in a restaurant. He seemed relieved and said, 'I would never have dared to take the first step.' He was shaken for two or three days, then recovered nicely. As he put it, he 'supported celibacy' quite effortlessly. It felt natural to him, it was his natural condition.

I went to New York for a week. By chance he went there after I returned. When we saw each other again in Paris we were as awkward as adolescents. His allergies were acting up; American food had made him put on two kilos; a New York barber had thrown his meaty ears into high relief. 'It's terrible,' Jean-Loup said, 'I wanted my independence, but now that I have it . . . Undress me.' I did so, triumphant while registering his admission that he was the one after all who had wanted to be free.

After that we saw each other seldom but when we did it was always passionate. The more people we told that we were no longer lovers, the more violent our desire for each other became. I found his heavy balls, which he liked me to hold in my mouth while I looked up at him. I found the mole on his smooth haunch. Because of his allergies he couldn't tolerate colognes or deodorants; I was left with his natural kid-brother smell. We had long passed through the stage of smoking marijuana together or using sex toys or dressing each other up in bits of finery. Other couples I knew became kinkier and kinkier over the years if they continued having sex or else resigned themselves to the most routine, suburban relief. We were devouring each other with a desire that was ever purer and sharper. Of course such a desire is seldom linked to love. It can be powerful when solicited but quickly forgotten when absent, since it may never have played a part in one's dreams of the future.

Perhaps the threat of ending things altogether, which we'd just averted, had made us keener. More likely, Jean-Loup, now that he thought he'd become less homosexual by shedding a male lover, me, felt freer to indulge drives that had become more urgent precisely because they were less well defined. Or perhaps I'm exaggerating my importance in his eyes; as he once said, he didn't like to wank his head over things like that ('*Je ne me branle pas trop la tête*').

I was in love with him and, during sex, thought of that love, but I tried to conceal it from him.

I tried to expect nothing, see him when I saw him, pursue other men, as though I were strictly alone in the world. For the first time when he asked me if I had other lovers I said I did and even discussed them with him. He said he was relieved, explaining that my adventures exonerated him from feeling responsible for me and my happiness. He was a lousy lover, he said, famous for being elusive; even his girl-friends complained about his slipperiness. That elusiveness, I would discover, was his protest against his own passivity, his longing to be owned.

Things changed day by day between us. He said he wasn't searching for other sexual partners; he preferred to wait until he fell in love, revealing that he didn't see us becoming lovers again. Nor was he in such a hurry to find a distinguished and sympathetic slut for a wife. When I asked him about his marital plans, he said that he was still looking forward to settling down with a wife and children some day but that now he recognized that when he thought of rough sex, of *la baise harde*, he thought of men. And again he flatteringly blamed me for having corrupted him even while he admitted he was looking for someone else, another man, to love.

Once in a very great while he referred to me playfully as his 'husband', despite his revulsion against camp. I think he was trying to come up with a way that would let our friendship continue while giving each of us permission to pursue other people. Once he sombrely spoke of me as his *patron* but I winced and he quickly withdrew the description. I wouldn't have minded playing his father, but that never occurred to him.

I'm afraid I'm making him sound too cold. He also had a sweet kid-brother charm, especially around women. All those former débutantes from Bordeaux living in Paris felt free to ask him to run an errand or install a bookcase, which he did with unreflecting devotion. He was careful (far more careful than any American would have been) to distinguish between a pal and a friend, but the true friends exercised an almost limitless power over him. Jean-Loup was quite proud of his capacity for friendship. When he would say that he was a rotten lover—elusive, unsure of his direction—he'd also assure me that he'd always remain my faithful friend, and I believed him. I knew that he was, in fact, waiting for our passion to wear itself out so that a more decent friendship could declare itself.

He wasn't a friend during sex or just afterwards, he'd always shower, dress and leave as quickly as possible. Once, when he glanced back at the rubble we had made of the bedroom, he said all that evidence of our bestiality disgusted him. Nor was he specially kind to me around our playmates. To them, paradoxically, he enjoyed demonstrating how thoroughly he was at home in my apartment. He was the little lord of the manor. Yet he'd compliment me on how well I 'received' people and assure me I could always open a restaurant in New York some day if my career as a writer petered out. He didn't take my writing too seriously. It had shocked him the few times he'd dipped into it. He preferred the lucidity and humanism of Milan Kundera, his favourite writer. In fact none of our playmates read me, and their indifference pleased me. It left me alone with my wet sand.

He took a reserved interest in my health. He was relieved that my blood tests every six months suggested the virus was still dormant. He was pleased I no longer smoked or drank (though like most French people he didn't consider champagne alcoholic). During one of our sex games he poured half a bottle of red Sancerre down my throat; the etiquette of the situation forbade my refusal, but it was the only time I had tasted alcohol in nearly ten years. We were convinced that the sort of sex we practised might be demented but was surely safe; in fact we had made it demented since it had to stay safe.

He was negative. While he waited for his results, he said that if they turned out positive his greatest regret would be that he wouldn't be able to father children. A future without a family seemed unbearable. As long as his boy's body with its beautifully shaped man's penis remained unmarked, without a sign of its past or a curse over its future, he was happy to lend himself to our games.

Sometimes his laugh was like a shout—boyish, the sound, but the significance, knowing Parisian. He laughed to show that he hadn't been taken in or that he had caught the wicked allusion. When I was in the kitchen preparing the next course, I'd smile if I heard his whoop. I liked it that he was my husband, so at home, so sociable, so light-hearted, but our marriage was just a poor invention of my own fancy.

It reassured me that his sexuality was profoundly, not modishly, violent. He told me that when he had been a child, just seven or eight, he had built a little town out of cardboard and plywood, painted every shutter and peopled every house, and then set the whole construction afire and watched the conflagration with a bone-hard, inch-long erection. Is that why just touching me made him hard now (bone-hard, foot-long)? Could he see I was ablaze with ardour for him (ardour with a silent *h*)?

The violence showed up again in the comic strips he was always drawing. He had invented a sort of Frankenstein monster in good French clothes, a creature disturbed by his own half-human sentiments in a world otherwise populated by robots. When I related his comics to the history of art, he'd smile a gay, humiliated smile, the premonitory form of his whooping, disabused Parisian laugh. He was ashamed I made so much of his talent, though his talent was real enough.

He didn't know what to do with his life. He was living as ambitious, healthy young men live who have long vistas of time before them: despairingly. I, who had already outlived my friends and had fulfilled some of my hopes but few of my desires (desire won't stay satisfied), lived each day with joy and anguish. Jean-Loup expected his life to be perfect: there was apparently going to be so much of it.

Have I mentioned that Jean-Loup had such high arches that walking hurt him? He had one of his feet broken, lowered and screwed shut in metal vices that were removed six months later. His main reason for the operation was to escape the bank for a few weeks. His clinic room was soon snowed under with comic strip adventures. After that he walked with a bit of a Chaplinesque limp when he was tired.

I often wondered what his life was like with the other young Bordelais counts and countesses at Saint Jean-de-Luz every August. I was excluded from that world—the chance of my being introduced to his childhood friends had never even once entered his head—which made me feel like a *demi-mondaine* listening avidly to her titled young lover's accounts of his exploits in the great world. Although I presented Jean-Loup to my literary friends in London, he had few opinions about them beyond his admiration for the men's clothes and the women's beauty and apparent intelligence. 'It was all so fast and brilliant,' he said, 'I scarcely understood a word.' He blamed me for not helping him with his English, though he hated the sounds I made when I spoke my native language. 'You don't have an accent in French—oh, you have your little accent, but it's nothing, very charming. But in American you sound like a duck, it's frightful!'

I suppose my English friends thought it was a sentimental autumn-and-spring affair. One friend, who lent us her London house for a few days, said, 'Don't let the char see you and Jean-Loup nude.' I thought the warning seemed bizarre until I understood it as an acknowledgement of our potential for sensual mischief. Perhaps she was particularly alive to sensual possibilities, since she was so proud of her own handsome, young husband.

After I returned to Paris, I spent my days alone reading and writing, and in fair weather I'd eat a sandwich on the quay. That January the Seine overflowed and flooded the highway on the Right Bank. Seagulls flew upstream and wheeled above the turbulent river, crying, as though mistaking Notre Dame for Mont-St Michel. The floodlights trained on the church's façade projected ghostly shadows of the two square towers up into the foggy night sky, as though spirits were doing axonometric drawings of a cathedral I had always thought of as malign. The gargoyles were supposed to ward off evil, but to me they looked like dogs straining to leap away from the devil comfortably lodged within.

I went to Australia and New Zealand for five weeks. I wrote Jean-Loup many letters, in French, believing that the French language tolerated love better than English, but when I returned to Paris Jean-Loup complained of my style. He found it 'mièvre', 'wimpy' or 'wet'.

He said I should write about his ass one day, but in a style that was neither pornographic nor wimpy. He wanted me to describe his ass as Francis Ponge describes soap: an objective, exhaustive, whimsical catalogue of its properties.

I wanted someone else, but I distrusted that impulse, because it seemed, if I looked back, I could see that I had never been happy in love and that with Jean-Loup I was happier than usual. As he pointed out, we were still having sex after two years, and he ascribed the intensity to the very infrequency that I deplored. Even so, I thought there was something all wrong, fundamentally wrong, with me: I set up a lover as a god, then burned with rage when he proved mortal. I lay awake, next to one lover after another, in a rage, dreaming of someone who'd appreciate me, give me the simple affection I imagined I wanted.

When I broke off with Jean-Loup over dinner he said, 'You deserve someone better, someone who will love you completely.' Yet the few times I had been loved 'completely' I felt suffocated. Nor could I imagine a less aristocratic lover, one who'd sit beside me on the couch, hand in hand, and discuss the loft bed, the 'mezzanine', we should buy with the cunning little chair and matching desk underneath.

But when I was alone night after night, I resented Jean-Loup's independence. He said I deserved something better, and I knew I merited less but needed more.

It was then I saw the redhead at the reading. Although I stared holes through him, he never looked at me once. It occurred to me that he might not be homosexual, except that his grave military bearing was something only homosexuals could (or would bother to) contrive if they weren't actually soldiers. His whole look and manner were studied. Let's say he was the sort of homosexual other homosexuals recognize but that heterosexuals never suspect.

The next day I asked the owner of the bookstore if she knew the redhead. 'He comes into the shop every so often,' she said, with a quick laugh to acknowledge the character of my curiosity, 'but I don't know his name. He bought one of your books. Perhaps he'll come to your reading next week.'

I told her to be sure to get his name if he returned. 'You were a diplomat once,' I reminded her. She promised but when I phoned a few days later she said he hadn't been in. Then on the night of my reading I saw him sitting in the same chair as before and I went up to him with absolute confidence and said, 'I'm so glad you came tonight. I saw you at the last reading, and my *copine* and I thought you looked so interesting we wished we knew you.' He looked so blank that I was afraid he hadn't understood and I almost started again in French. I introduced myself and shook his hand. He went white and said, 'I'm sorry for not standing up,' and then stood up and shook my hand, and I was afraid he'd address me as 'sir'.

Now that I could look at his hair closely I noticed that it was blond, if shavings of gold are blond, only on the closely cropped sides but that it was red on top—the reverse of the sun-bleached strawberry blond. He gave me his phone number, and I thought this was someone I could spend the rest of my life with, however brief that might be. His name was Paul.

I phoned him the next day to invite him to dinner, and he said that he had a rather strange schedule, since he worked four nights a week for a disco.

'What do you do?' I asked.

'I'm the physiognomist. The person who recognizes the regulars and the celebrities. I have to know what Brigitte Bardot looks like *now*. I decide who comes in, who stays out, who pays, who doesn't. We have a house rule to let all models in free.' He told me people called him Cerberus.

'But how do you recognize everyone?'

'I've been on the door since the club opened seven years ago. So I have ten thousand faces stored in my memory.' He laughed. 'That's why I could never move back to America. I'd never find a job that paid so well for just twenty hours' work a week. And in America I couldn't do the same job, since I don't know any faces there.'

We arranged an evening and he arrived dressed in clothes by one of the designers he knew from the club. Not even my reactionary father, however, would have considered him a popinjay. He did nothing that would risk his considerable dignity. He had white tulips in his surprisingly small, elegant hand.

All evening we talked literature, and, as two good Americans, we also exchanged confidences. Sometimes his shyness brought all the laughter and words to a queasy halt, and it made me think of that becalmed moment when a sailboat comes around and the mainsail luffs before it catches the wind again. I watched the silence play over his features.

He was from a small town in Georgia. His older brother and he had each achieved highest score in the state-wide scholastic aptitude test. They had not pulled down good grades, however; they read Plato and *Naked Lunch*, staged *No Exit* and brawls with the boys in the next town, experimented with hallucinogens and conceptual art. Paul's brother made an 'art work' out of his plans to assassinate President Ford and was arrested by the FBI.

'I just received the invitation to my tenth high-school reunion,' Paul said.

'I'll go with you,' I said. 'I'll go as your spouse.'

He looked at me and breathed a laugh, save it was voiced just at the end, the moving bow finally touching the bass string and waking sound in it.

Paul's older brother had started a rock band, gone off to New York, where he died of AIDS—another musician punished. He had been one of the first heterosexual male victims—dead already in 1981. He contracted the disease from a shared needle. Their mother, a Scottish immigrant, preferred to think he had been infected by another man. Love seemed a nobler cause of death than drugs.

'Then I came to Paris,' Paul said. He sighed and looked out of my open window at the roofs of the Ile St Louis. Like other brilliant young men and women he suspended every solid in a solution of irony, but even he had certain articles of faith, and the first was Paris. He liked French manners, French clothes, French food, French education. He said things like, 'France still maintains cultural hegemony over the whole world,' and pronounced 'hegemony' as '*hégémonie*'. He had done all his studies as an adult in France and French. He asked me what the name of *Platon*'s *Le Banquet* was in English (*The Symposium*, for some reason). He had a lively, but somewhat vain, sense of what made him interesting, which struck me only because he seemed so worthy of respect that any attempt to serve himself up appeared irrelevant.

He was wearing a white shirt and dark tie and military shoes and a beautiful dark jacket that was cut to his Herculean chest and shoulders. He had clear eyes, pale blue eyes. The white tulips he brought were waxen and pulsing like lit candles, and his skin, that rich hairless skin, was tawny-coloured. His manners were formal and French, a nice Georgia boy but Europeanized, someone who'd let me lazily finish my sentences in French ('*quand même*,' we'd say, '*rien à voir avec* . . .'). His teeth were so chalky white that the red wine stained them a faint blue.

His face was at once open and unreadable, as imposing as the globe. He nodded slowly as he thought over what I said, so slowly that I doubted the truth or seriousness of what I was saying. He hesitated and his gaze was non-committal, making me wonder if he was pondering his own response or simply panicking. I wouldn't have thought of him panicking except he mentioned it. He said he was always on the edge of panic (the sort of thing Americans say to each other with big grins). Points of sweat danced on the bridge of his nose, and I thought I saw in his eye something frightened, even unpleasant and unreachable. I kept thinking we were too much alike, as though at any moment our American heartiness and our French *politesse* would break down and we'd look at each other with the sour familiarity of brothers. Did he sense it, too? Is that why our formality was so important to him? I was sure he hadn't liked himself in America.

Speaking French so long had made me simplify my thoughts— whether expressed in French or English—and I was pleased I could say now what I felt, since the intelligence I was imputing to him would never have tolerated my old vagueness. Whereas Jean-Loup had insisted I use the right fork, I felt Paul would insist on the correct emotion.

Sometimes before he spoke Paul made a faint humming sound—perhaps only voiced shyness—but it gave the impression of the slightest deference. It made me think of a student half-raising his hand to talk to a seminar too small and egalitarian to require the teacher's recognition to speak. But I also found myself imagining that his thought was so varied, occurring on so many levels at once that the hum was a strictly mechanical downshift into the compromise (and invention) of speech. After a while the hum disappeared, and I fancied he felt more at ease with me, although the danger is always to read too much into what handsome men say and do. Although he was twenty years younger, he seemed much older than me.

'Would you like to go to Morocco with me?' I asked him

suddenly. 'For a week? A magazine will pay our fares. It's the south of Morocco. It should be amusing. I don't know it at all, but I think it's better to go somewhere brand new—' ('with a lover' were the words I suppressed).

'Sure.'

He said he hadn't travelled anywhere in Europe or Africa except for two trips to Italy.

Although I knew things can't be rushed, that intimacy follows its own sequence, I found myself saying, 'We should be lovers— you have everything, beauty and intelligence.' Then I added: 'And we get on so well.' My reasoning was absurd: his beauty and intelligence were precisely what made him unavailable.

I scarcely wanted him to reply. As long as he didn't I could nurse my illusions. 'That would depend,' he said, 'on our being compatible sexually, don't you think?' Then he asked, with his unblinking gravity, 'What's your sexuality like?' For the first time I could hear a faint Georgia accent in the way the syllables of *sexuality* got stretched out.

'It depends on the person,' I said, stalling. Then, finding my answer lamentable, I pushed all my chips forward on one number: 'I like pain.'

'So do I,' he said. 'And my penis has never—no man has ever touched it.'

He had had only three lovers and they had all been heterosexuals or fancied they were. In any event they had had his sort of *pudeur* about using endearments to another man. He had a lover now, Thierry, someone he met two years before at the club. The first time they saw each other, Paul had been tanked up on booze, smack and steroids, a murderous cocktail, and they had a fist-fight which had dissolved into a night of violent passion.

Every moment must have been haloed in his memory, for he remembered key phrases Thierry had used. For the last two years they had eaten every meal together. Thierry dressed him in the evening before Paul left for work and corrected his French and table manners. These interventions were often nasty, sometimes violent. 'What language are you speaking now?' he would demand

74

if Paul made the slightest error. When Paul asked for a little tenderness in bed, Thierry would say, 'Oh-ho, like Mama and Papa now, is it?' and then leave the room. Paul fought back—he broke his hand once because he hit Thierry so hard. 'Of course *he'd* say that it was all my fault,' Paul said, 'that all he wants is peace, blue skies.' He smiled. 'Thierry is a businessman, very dignified. He has never owned a piece of leather in his life. I despise leather. It robs violence of all the'—his smile now radiant, the mainsail creaking as it comes around—'the *sacramental*.' He laughed, shaking, and made a strange chortle that I didn't really understand. It came out of a sensibility I hadn't glimpsed in him before.

Paul longed for us to reach the desert; he had never seen it before.

    We started out at Agadir and took a taxi to the mud-walled town of Taroudannt. There we hired a car and drove to Ouarzazate, which had been spoiled by organized tourism: it had become Anywhere Sunny. Then we drove south to Zagora. It was just twenty kilometres beyond Zagora, people said, that the desert started. I warned Paul the desert could be disappointing: 'You're never alone. There's always someone spying on you from over the next dune. And it rains. I saw the rain pour over Syria.'

Paul loved maps. Sometimes I could see in him the solitary Georgia genius in love with his best friend's father, the sheriff, a kid lurking around home in the hot, shuttered afternoons, day-dreaming over the globe that his head so resembled, his mind racing on home-made LSD. He knew how to refold maps, but when they were open he would press his palms over their creases as though opening his own eyes wider and wider.

I did all the driving, through adobe cities built along narrow, palm-lined roads. In every town boys wanted to be our guides, sell us trinkets or carpets or their own bodies. They hissed at us at night from the shadows of town walls: lean and finely muscled adolescents hissing to attract our attention, their brown hands massaging a lump beneath the flowing blue acrylic *jellabias* mass-produced in China. To pass them up with a smile was a new experience for me. I had Paul beside me, this noble pacing lion. I remembered a Paris friend calling me just before we left for

Morocco, saying he had written a letter to a friend, 'telling him I'd seen you walking down the boulevard St Germain beside the young Hercules with hair the colour of copper.' In Morocco there was no one big enough, powerful enough or cruel enough to interest Paul.

Perhaps it was due to the clear, memorable way Paul had defined his sexual nature, but during our cold nights together I lay in his great arms and never once felt excited, just an immense feeling of peace and gratitude. Our predicament, we felt, was like a Greek myth. 'Two people love each other,' I said, 'but the gods have cursed them by giving them the identical passions.' I was being presumptuous, sneaking in the phrase, 'Two people love each other,' because it wasn't at all clear that he loved me.

One night we went to the movies and saw an Italian adventure film starring American weight-lifters and dubbed in French, a story set in a back-lot castle with a perfunctory princess in hot pants. There was an evil prince whose handsome face melted to reveal the devil's underneath. His victim ('All heroes are masochists,' Paul declared) was an awkward body-builder not yet comfortable in his newly acquired bulk, who had challenged the evil prince's supremacy and now must be flayed alive. Paul clapped and chortled and, during the tense scenes, physically braced himself. This was the Paul who had explained what Derrida had said of Heidegger's interpretation of Trakl's last poems, who claimed that literature could be studied only through rhetoric, grammar and genre, and who considered Ronsard a greater poet than Shakespeare (because of Ronsard's combination of passion and logic, satyr and god, in place of the mere conversational fluency which Paul regarded as the flaw and genius of English): this was the same Paul who booed and cheered as the villain smote the hero before a respectful audience thick with smoke and the flickers of flashlights. It was a movie in which big men were hurting each other.

Jean-Loup would have snorted, his worst prejudices about Americans confirmed, for as we travelled, drawing closer and closer to the desert, we confided more and more in each other. As we drove through the 'valley of a thousand casbahs', Paul told me about threats to his life. 'When someone at the club pulls a gun on me, and it's happened three times, I say, I'm sorry but guns are not permitted on the premises, and it works, they go away, but mine is a suicidal response.' Paul was someone on whom nothing was wasted: nevertheless sometimes he was not always alive to all possibilities, at least not instantly. I told him I was positive, but he didn't react. Behind the extremely dark sun-glasses, there was this presence, breathing and thinking but not reacting.

Our hotel, the Hesperides, had been built into the sun-baked mud ramparts in the ruins of the pasha's palace. We stared into an octagonal, palm-shaded pool glistening with black rocks that then slid and clicked—ah, tortoises! There couldn't have been more than five guests, and the porters, bored and curious, tripped over themselves serving us. We slept in each other's arms night after night and I stroked his great body as though he were a prize animal, *la belle bête*. My own sense of who I was in this story was highly unstable. I flickered back and forth, wanting to be the blond warrior's fleshy, harem-pale concubine or then the bearded pasha himself, feeding drugged sherberts to the beautiful Circassian slave I had bought. I thought seriously that I wouldn't mind buying and owning another human being—if it were Paul.

The next day we picked up some hitch-hikers who, when we reached their destination, asked us in for mint tea, which we sipped barefoot in a richly carpeted room. A baby and a chicken watched us through the doorway from the sun-white courtyard. Every one of our encounters seemed to end with a carpet, usually one we were supposed to buy. In a village called Wodz, I remember both of us smiling as we observed how long and devious the path to the carpet could become: there was first a tourist excursion through miles of casbah, nearly abandoned except for an old veiled woman poking a fire in a now roofless harem; then we took a stroll through an irrigated palm plantation, where a woman leading a donkey took off her turban, a blue bath-towel, and filled it with dates which she gave us, with a golden grin; and finally we paid a 'surprise visit' on the guide's 'brother', the carpet merchant who happened to have just returned from the desert with exotic Tuareg rugs whose prices, to emphasize their exoticism, he pretended to translate from Tuareg dollars into dirham.

We laughed, bargained, bought, happy any time our shoulders touched or eyes met. We told everyone we were Danes, since this was the one language even the most resourceful carpet merchants didn't know ('But wait, I have a cousin in the next village who once lived in Copenhagen').

Later, when I returned to Paris, I would discover that Jean-Loup had left me for Régis, one of the richest men in France. For the first time in his life he was in love, he would say. He would be wearing Régis's wedding-ring, my Jean-Loup who had refused to stay behind at my apartment after the other guests had left lest he appear too *pédé*. People would suspect him of being interested in the limousine, the town house, the château, but Jean-Loup would insist it was all love.

When he told me, on my return, that he would never sleep with me again—that he had found the man with whom he wanted to spend the rest of his life—my response surprised him. '*Ça tombe bien,*' I said ('That suits the situation perfectly').

Jean-Loup blurted out: 'But you're supposed to be furious.'

It wasn't that he wanted me to fight to get him back, though he might have enjoyed it, but that his vanity demanded that I protest: my own vanity made me concede him with a smile. Feverishly I filled him in on my recent passion for Paul and the strategies I had devised for unloading him, Jean-Loup. It's true I had tried to fix him up a week earlier with a well-heeled, handsome young American.

Jean-Loup's eyes widened. 'I had no idea,' he said, 'that things had gone so far.' Perhaps in revenge he told me how he had met Régis. It seems that, while I was away, a dear mutual friend had fixed them up.

I was suddenly furious and couldn't drop the subject. I railed and railed against the dear mutual friend: 'When I think he ate my food, drank my drink, all the while plotting to marry you off to a millionaire in order to advance his own miserable little interests . . .'

'Let me remind you that Régis's money means nothing to me. No, what I like is his good humour, his sincerity, his discretion. It was hard for me to be known as your lover—your homosexuality is too evident. Régis is very discreet.'

'What rubbish,' I would say a few days later when Jean-Loup repeated the remark about Régis's discretion. 'He's famous for surrounding himself with aunties who talk lace prices the livelong day.'

'Ah,' Jean-Loup replied, reassured, 'you've been filled in, I see' ('*Tu t'en renseignes*').

All sparkling and droll, except a terrible sickness, like an infection caused by the prick of a diamond brooch, had set in. When I realized that I would never be able to abandon myself again to Jean-Loup's perverse needs, when I thought that Régis was enjoying the marriage with him I'd reconciled myself never to know, when I saw the serenity with which Jean-Loup now 'assumed' his homosexuality, I felt myself sinking, but genuinely sinking, as though I really were falling, and my face had a permanently hot blush. I described this feeling of falling and heat to Paul. 'That's jealousy,' he said. 'You're jealous.' That must be it, I thought, I who had never been jealous before. If I had behaved so generously with earlier loves lost it was because I had never before been consumed by sensuality this feverish.

Jealousy, yes, it was jealousy, and never before had I so wanted to hurt someone I loved, and that humiliated me further. A member of the play-pen dined at Régis's *hôtel particulier*. 'They hold hands all the time,' she said. 'I was agreeably surprised by Régis, a charming man. The house is more a museum than a . . . house. Jean-Loup kept calling the butler for more champagne, and we almost burst out laughing. It was like a dream.'

Every detail fed my rancour—Régis's charm, wealth, looks ('Not handsome but attractive').

Everything.

Paul had a photographic memory, and, during the hours spent together in the car in Morocco, he recited page after page of Racine or Ronsard or Sir Philip Sidney. He also continued the story of his life. I wanted to know every detail—the bloody scenes on the steps of the disco, the recourse to dangerous drugs, so despised by the clenched-jaw cocaine set. I wanted to hear that he credited his lover with saving him from being a junkie, a drunk and a thug. 'He was the one who got me back into school.'

'A master, I see,' I thought. '*School* master.'

'Now I study *Ciceron* and prepare my *maîtrise*, but then I was just an animal, a disoriented bull—I'd even gotten into beating up fags down by the Seine at dawn when I was really drunk.'

He gave me a story he had written. It was Hellenistic in tone, precious and edgy, flirting with the diffuse lushness of a pre-Raphaelite prose, rich but bleached, like a tapestry left out in the sun. I suppose he must have had in mind Mallarmé's *The Prelude to the Afternoon of a Faun*, but Paul's story was more touching, less cold, more comprehensible. That such a story could never be published in the minimalist, plain-speaking 1980s seemed never to have occurred to him. Could it be that housed in such a massive body he had no need for indirect proofs of power and accomplishment? Or was he so sure of his taste that recognition scarcely interested him at all?

The story is slow to name its characters, but begins with a woman who turns out to be Athena. She's discovering the flute and how to get music out of it, but her sisters, seeing her puffing away, laugh at the face she's making. Athena throws the flute down and in a rage places a curse on it: 'Whoever would make use of it next must die.' Her humiliation would cost a life.

The next user is a cheerful satyr named Marsyas. He cleverly learns how to imitate people with his tunes: 'Prancing along behind them he could do their walk, fast or slow, lurching or clipped, just as he could render their tics or trace their contours: a low swell for a belly, shrill fifing for fluttering hands, held high notes for the adagio of soft speech. At first no one understood. But once they caught on they slapped their thighs: his songs were sketches.'

Apollo is furious, since he's the god of music and his own art is pure and abstract. He challenges Marsyas to a musical duel:

> Marsyas cringed before them like a dog when it walks
> through a ghost, bares its teeth and pulls back its ears.
> Anguished, he had slept in the hot breath of his flock; his
> animals had pressed up against him, holding him between
> their woolly flanks, as though to warm him. The ribbon
> his jolly and jiggling woman had tied around one horn

flapped listlessly against his low, hairy brow, like a royal banner flown by a worker's barge.

To the gods, as young as the morning, Marsyas seemed a twilit creature; he smelled of leaf mould and wolf-lair. His glance was as serious as a deer's when it emerges from the forest at dusk to drink at the calm pool collecting below a steaming cataract.

And to Marsyas his rival was cold and regular as cambered marble.

Since Marsyas knew to play only what was in front of him, he 'rendered' Apollo—not the god's thoughts but the faults he wedged into the air around him. The sisters watched the goat-man breathe into the reeds, saw him draw and lose breath, saw his eyes bulge, brown and brilliant as honey, and that made them laugh. What they heard, however, was colours that copied sacred lines, for Marsyas could imitate a god as easily as a bawd. The only trick was to have his model there, in front of him.

If Marsyas gave them the god's form, the god himself revealed the contents of his mind. His broad hand swept up the lyre, and immediately the air was tuned and the planets tempered. Everything sympathetic trembled in response to a song that took no one into account, that moved without moving, that polished crystal with its breath alone, clouding then cleansing every transparency without touching it. Marsyas shuddered when he came to and realized that the god's hand was now motionless but that the music continued to devolve, creaking like a finger turning and tracing the fragile rim of the spheres.

The satyr was astonished that the goddesses didn't decide instantly in their brother's favour but shrugged and smiled and said they found each contestant appealing in different ways. The sun brightened a fraction with Apollo's anger, but then the god suggested they each play their music backwards. The universe shuddered as it stopped and reversed its rotations; the sun started to descend toward dawn as Apollo unstrung the planets. Cocks re-crowed and bats re-awakened, the frightened shepherd guided his flock back down the hill as the dew fell again.

Even the muses were frightened. It was night and stormy when Marsyas began to play. He had improvised his music strophe by strophe as a portrait; now he couldn't remember it all. The descending figures, so languishing when played correctly the first time, made him queasy when he inverted them. Nor could he see his subject.

The muses decided in the god's favour. Apollo told Marsyas he'd be flayed alive. There was no tenderness but great solicitude in the way the god tied the rope around the satyr's withers, cast the slack over a high branch of a pine and then hoisted his kill high, upside down, inverted as the winning melody. Marsyas saw that he'd won the god's full attention by becoming his victim.

The blood ran to Marsyas's head, then spurted over his chest as Apollo sliced into his belly, neatly peeled back the flesh and fat and hair. The light shone in rays from Apollo's sapphire eyes and locked with Marsyas's eyes, which were wavering, losing grip—he could feel his eyes lose grip, just as a child falling asleep will finally relax its hold on its father's finger. A little dog beside his head was lapping up the fresh blood. Now the god knelt to continue his task. Marsyas could hear the quick sharp breaths, for killing him was hard work. The God's white skin glowed and the satyr believed he was inspiring the very breath Apollo expired.

As I read his story I stupidly wondered which character Paul was—the Apollo he so resembled and whose abstract ideal of art appeared to be his own, or the satyr who embodies the vital principle of mimesis and who, after all, submitted to the god's cruel, concentrated attention. The usual motive for the story, Apollo's jealousy, was left out altogether, as though pique were an emotion Paul didn't know (certainly he hadn't shown any in eight days on the road). His story was dedicated to me, and for a moment I wondered if it were also addressed to me—as a reproach for having abandoned the Apollonian abstractness of my first two novels or, on the contrary, as an endorsement for undertaking my later satires and sketches? It was unsettling dealing with this young man so brilliant and handsome, so violent and so reflective.

At night Paul let me into his bed and held me in his arms, just as he sometimes rested his hand on my leg as I drove the car. He told me that, although Thierry often petted him, Paul was never allowed to stroke him. 'We've never once kissed each other on the lips.'

We talked skittishly about the curse the gods had put on us. I pathetically attempted to persuade Paul he was really a sadist. 'Your invariable rage after sex with your lover,' I declared, melodramatically, 'your indignation, your disgusting excursions into fag-bashing, your primitive, literalist belief that only the biggest man with the biggest penis has the right to dominate all the others, whereas the sole glory of sadism is its strictly cerebral capacity for imposing new values, your obvious attraction to my fundamentally docile nature'—and at that point my charlatanism would make me burst out laughing, even as I glanced sideways to see how I was doing.

In fact my masochism sickened him. It reminded him of his own longing to recapture Thierry's love. 'He left me,' he would say. 'When calls come in he turns the sound off on the answering machine and he never replays his messages when I'm around. His pockets bulge with condoms. He spends every weekend with purely fictive "German businessmen" in Normandy; he pretends he's going to visit a factory in Nice, but he's back in Paris four hours later; he stood me up for the Mister Body-building contest at the Parc de Vincennes then was seen there with a famous Brazilian model . . . He says I should see a psychiatrist, and you know how loony someone French must think you are to suggest that.'

When a thoughtful silence had re-established itself in the car I added, 'That's why you want to reach the desert. Only its vast sterility can calm your violent soul.'

'If you could be in my head,' he said, not smiling, 'you'd see I'm in a constant panic.'

To be companionable I said, 'Me too.'

Paul quickly contradicted me: 'But you're the calmest person I know.'

Then I understood that was how he wanted me to be— masterful, confident, smiling, sure. Even if he would some day dominate, even hurt me, as I wished, he would never give me permission to suffer in any way except heroically.

I drove a few miles in silence through the lunar valley, mountains on both sides, not yet the desert but a coarse-grained prelude to it—dry, gently rolling, the boulders the colour of egg-plants. 'You're right, except so many of the people I've known have died. The way we talk, you and me, about books and life and love. I used to talk this way with my best friend, but that was in America and now he is dead.' That night, in Paul's arms, I said, 'It's sacrilegious to say it, especially for an atheist, but I feel God sent you not to replace my friend, since he's irreplaceable, but . . .'

A carpet salesman assured us the desert was about to begin. We had been following a river through the valley, and at last it had run dry, and the date palms had vanished, and the mountains knelt like camels just before setting out on a long journey. In Zagora we saw the famous sign, 'Timbuctoo: 54 days.' In a village we stopped to visit the seventeenth-century library of a saint, Abu Abdallah Mohammed Bennacer, a small room of varnished wood cases beside a walled-in herbal garden. The old guide in his white robes opened for us—his hands were wood-hard—some of the illustrated volumes, including a Koran written on gazelle skin. Paul's red hair and massive body made him rarer than a gazelle in this dusty village. That night a village boy asked me if I had a 'gazelle' back in Paris, and I figured out he meant a girl-friend and nodded because that was the most efficient way to stanch a carpet-tending spiel.

Paul continued with his stories. The one about the French woman he had loved and married off to the paratrooper, who had already become his lover. The one about the Los Angeles sadist he ridiculed and who then committed suicide. About his second date with Thierry, when he'd been gagged and chained upside down in a dungeon after being stuffed with acid, then made to face a huge poster of the dead L.A. lover. The one about the paratrooper scaling the mountain at the French-Italian border while cops in circling helicopters ordered him to descend immediately—'and applauded in spite of themselves when he reached the top bare-handed,' Paul exulted, 'without a rope or pick or anything to scale the sheer rock face but balls and brawn.'

We're too alike, I thought again, despairing, to love each other, and Paul is different only in his attraction to cartoon images of male violence and aggression. Unlike him, I couldn't submit to a psychopath; what I want is Paul, with all his tenderness and quizzical, hesitating intelligence, his delicacy, to hit me. To be hurt by an enraged bull on steroids doesn't excite me. What I want is to belong to this grave, divided, philosophical man.

It occurred to me that if I thought only now, at this moment in my life, of belonging to someone, it was because my hold on life itself was endangered. Did I want him to tattoo his initials on a body I might soon have to give up? Did I want to become his slave just before I embraced that lasting solitude?

The beginning of the desert was a dune that had drifted through the pass between two mountains and had started to fill up the scrub-land. A camel with bald spots on its elbows and starlet eyelashes was tethered to a dark felt tent in which a dirty man was sprawling, half-asleep. Another man, beaming and freshly shaved, bustled out of a cement bunker. With a flourish he invited us in for a glass of mint tea. His house turned out to be a major carpet showroom, buzzing with air-conditioning and neon lamps. 'English?'

'No. Danish.'

That was the last night of our holiday. The hotel served us a feast of sugared pigeon pie and mutton couscous, and Paul had a lot to drink. We sat in the dark beside the pool, which was lit from within like a philosopher's stone. He told me he thought of me as 'gay' in the Nietzschean, not the West Hollywood, sense, but since I insisted that I needed him, he would love me and protect me and spend his life with me. Later in bed he pounded me in the face with his fists, shouting at me in a stuttering, broken explosion of French and English, the alternately choked and released patois of scalding indignation.

If the great pleasure of the poor, or so they say, is making love, then the great suffering of the rich is loving in vain. The troubadours, who speak for their rich masters, are constantly reminding us that only men of refinement recognize the nobility of hopeless love; the vulgar crowd jeers at them for wasting their time. Only the idle and free can afford the luxury (the anguish) of making an absence into the very rose-heart of their lives. Only they have the extravagance of time to languish, shed tears, exalt their pain into poetry. For others time is too regulated; every day repeats itself.

I wasn't rich, but I was free and idle enough to ornament my liberty with the melancholy pleasure of having lost a Bordeaux boy with a claret-red mouth. All the while I'd been with Jean-Loup I'd admitted how ill-suited we were and I sought or dreamed of seeking someone else either tepidly or hotly, depending on the intensity of my dissatisfaction.

Now that Jean-Loup had left me for Régis, I could glorify their love and despise them and hate myself while sifting through my old memories to show myself that Jean-Loup had been slowly, if unconsciously, preparing this decampment for a long time.

When I am being wicked I tell people, 'Our little Jean-Loup has landed in clover. His worries are over. He's handed in his resignation at the bank. He'll soon be installed in the château for the summer and he can fill the moat with his *bandes dessinées*. The only pity is that Jean-Loup is apparently at Régis's mercy and Régis is cunning. He holds all the cards. If he tires of Jean-Loup, the poor boy will be dismissed without a centime, for that wedding-ring doesn't represent a claim, only a—'

But at this point bored, shocked friends laugh, hiss, 'Jealous, jealous, this way lies madness.' Jealousy may be new to me but not to them. My condition is as banal as it is baneful.

And then I realize that the opposite is probably true: that Jean-Loup had always dealt with me openly, even at the end, and had never resorted to subterfuge. As soon as he knew of his deep, innocent love for Régis he told me. I am the one who attributes scheming to him.

He always wanted me to describe his ass, so I'll conclude with an attempt not to sound too wet.

I should admit right off that by all ocular evidence there was nothing extraordinary about it. It wasn't a soccer player's muscled bum or a swimmer's sun-moulded twin *charlottes*. It was a kid brother's ass, a perfunctory transition between spine and legs, a simple cushion for a small body. Its colour was the low-wattage white of a winter half-moon. It served as the neutral support (as an anonymous glove supports a puppet's bobbing, expressive head) for his big, grown-up penis, always so ready to poke up through his flies and take centre-stage. But let's not hastily turn him around to reveal 'Régis's Daily Magic Baguette', as I now call it. No, let's keep his back to us, even though he's deliciously braced his knees to compensate for the sudden new weight he's cantilevered in his excitement, a heavy divining rod that makes his buttocks tense. Concave, each cheek looks glossy, like costly white satin that, having been stuffed in a drawer, has just been smoothed, thought it is still crazed with fine, whiter, silkier lines. If he spreads his cheeks—which feel cool, firm and plump—for the kneeling admirer, he reveals an anus that makes one think of a Leica lens, shut now but with many possible f-stops. An expensive aperture, but also a closed morning glory bud. There's that *grain de beauté* on his hip, the single drop of espresso on the wedding-gown. And there are the few silky hairs in the crack of his ass, wet now for some reason and plastered down at odd angles as though his fur had been greedily licked in all directions at once. If he spreads his legs and thinks about nothing—his fitting with the tailor, the castle drawbridge, the debs whose calls he can no longer return—his erection may melt and you might see it drooping lazily into view, just beyond his loosely bagged testicles. He told me that his mother would never let him sleep in his *slip* when he was growing up. She was afraid underpants might stunt his virile growth. These Bordeaux women know to let a young wine breathe.

GRANTA

TERESA PÀMIES
LETTERS TO MY
FATHER, NOW DEAD

1958

24 Ptrska Street
Prague

To my daughter Teresa,

I write to you with the following requests: To type out the pages I will be sending you from time to time and to make two copies. Not to change or add a thing of your own and not to improve on your father, bearing in mind that angels are not to be found on earth or in heaven. To ignore the bits of my writing that you can't read and not to worry about commas or full-stops.

Now that I've retired I have decided that I want to write about my life—not my whole life, not an autobiography, but those events that I've never really been able to digest before.

And so I, Tomás Pàmies Pla, born in 1889 in the town of Balaguer, now called Lérida, begin with an event that took place during Christmas in 1905, when I was sixteen years old. On our street, there was a poor, young widow with two children. Behind my father and elder brother's back, my mother used to help the young widow by washing her clothes, darning and giving her food. On Christmas day the widow fell ill and my mother said we must help her and asked me to make a collection for her. Together with the other boys of Balaguer, all of us more or less of peasant families, I went from door to door, filling large bags with food and clothes. And then we all went to the poor, young widow's house. When we stepped inside we were overwhelmed by what we saw. None of our families were at all well-off but never in our lives had

---

Tomás Pàmies fought for the communists in the Spanish Civil War and later worked for the Resistance in occupied France. He settled in Prague in 1953, working there as a gardener until his death in 1966. Tomas's daughter Teresa went to live in Prague after the death of her mother who drowned in the River Segre in Balaguer. Teresa moved to Paris before the Prague Spring and the Soviet invasion.

Opposite: Prague, 1968.

we seen such wretchedness. The little children were in a desperately weak state. They had never seen so much food and when they tried the first mouthful, one of them actually fainted. The mother, a good-looking woman though scarred by smallpox, seemed at that moment to be nothing but a pair of eyes. With a wisp of a voice she asked the children to thank us and she kissed our hands, tears streaming down her face.

I shall never forget the shame I felt when she kissed our hands. From that day onwards I've hated to see anyone kissing someone's hands.

Tomás

1968

Paris

Dear Father,

General Pavel was at your funeral, that melancholy-looking man who commanded the Czech brigade in the Civil War. I gave him my hand and he held it a moment, grasping it firmly. '*Salud*!' he said, the greeting we all used in Spain during the war. I introduced him to my brother and sister, and he looked at them as though he was hoping to find a common likeness in our three faces.

I was glad to see General Pavel at your funeral, father. He is a legendary figure in Czechoslovakia and not just because he fought in the International Brigade. He was taken at the same time as Slansky, Clementis and the others—the ones who were hanged in the fifties. You were not in Prague yet, but I was and witnessed it all. They couldn't hang Pavel because he refused to confess to being an agent of imperialism, as the others did at the trial. There were stories about him and he was said to be absolutely firm and full of courage. He wouldn't admit anything, and they couldn't prove the charges they had brought against him. They couldn't hang him.

General Pavel didn't go to your funeral in a black car, father. When the ceremony was over we saw him get on to a tram in the direction of Prikope. I was told that since he came out of prison he has been earning his living in a miserable clerical job with some publisher or foreign company.

I know you're not in the least happy that I keep telling you about General Pavel, ex-enemy of the working people, and if you could you'd shut me up in that characteristic way of yours, saying: 'That's enough from you.' But you are dead, father. We buried you in Prague on an October afternoon and it is essential that, dead and buried, you should listen to the story of people like Pavel, because things have happened that you could never have imagined, and had you been able to imagine them they'd have appalled you. And we have to talk about this. We, the dead and the living, must have the courage to see things as they are, come what may, though I or you or both of us die through doing so. Those who witnessed these things before were silent. I shall not be silent. And I do not want you to be silent, father, buried in Prague. And I shall call out to your tomb until you listen to me. And I shall wait in the rain and snow of Strashnice cemetery until you speak and tell me that you do not want to be silent either and that you will speak for me. With your heart in your hand.

Teresa

1959

24 Ptrska Street
Prague

To my daughter Teresa,

The very next summer, on 15 August 1906 to be precise (it was the Feast of the Assumption) I went to the house of the young widow with two young children. She had moved and was living in Calle de Abajo. When she opened the door, she said: 'I'm glad you've come, young man. It's my saint's day today and I'm by myself. I've got some cakes and coffee that my brother brought me yesterday when he came to take the children away. So we're alone.'

Her hair was loose, and as it was very hot she was wearing only a dressing-gown. I had brought her a parcel of clothes from my mother, and when the widow saw them she said she didn't need any clothes, things had changed and she even had a silk dressing-gown now. She added: 'Go on. Feel it, it's silk.' I felt it—it wasn't done up—and she moved so that I could feel her two breasts. It made me dizzy but I could not have lost my head altogether because I can still remember her leading me over to her bed. She must have realized the state I was in and guessed that she was the first woman I had ever had.

At four-thirty there was a knock at the door. The widow called out from the bed: 'Who is it?' and I heard my mother's voice say: 'It's La Teulera.' The widow answered very calmly: 'I'm sorry Rosa, but I'm having a wash. I'll come round when I've finished.' My mother insisted: 'Come and open the door—I've brought you a piece of meat pie.' And as the door was locked she added crossly: 'I'm leaving it on your doorstep. You can come over later.'

I was under the bed, trembling like a flan that had just been tipped out of its mould and when the widow gave me the sign I came out, quickly got dressed and ran home. I told my mother that I didn't feel well and that I'd been sick. She made me some camomile tea and packed me off to bed. I slept till the following morning.

Tomás

1960

24 Ptrska Street
Prague

To my daughter Teresa,

It was ten years before I married, and I was then working twelve to fourteen hours a day. I ignored my wife, and she accepted my treatment of her. She was very submissive. I'd spend a couple of minutes on top of her at night and then sleep like a log. I did not think of a wife as a companion; I did not even think of her as a citizen. I was ignorant. I did not know how to love, because loving is something you learn.

My wife must have suffered terribly. After eight months of marriage she died with a child in her womb. I had killed them both, out of ignorance. It was my first terrible blow. I fled all human contact. I returned to my parent's house and ended up staying in the orchard and not going to bed. Two friends of mine used to see me on Sundays and tell me how things were going in the European war. When I listened to them it was like hearing the rain fall. My mother made endless excuses for spending the day in the orchard, telling me stories about the family I had never heard before. That was how I learned that my grandfather had hanged himself and that my father had become impossible as a result.

Tomás

1968

Paris

Dear Father,

Do you realize that the day you died, 15 October, was St Teresa's day, which we used to celebrate at home with the St Teresa cakes mother made. Who would have imagined, when we were all together round the table, that you would die on St Teresa's day? I remember Mother preparing those cakes, soaking the slices of dry bread in a plate of sweetened milk the night before. Because my name is Teresa, she'd give me an extra one, and there were never any left for her. She'd say she wasn't hungry, that she'd nibbled as she went along, but that wasn't true. Mother always made excuses for giving us everything, with that gesture so characteristic of her, with something both sad and cheerful about it.

Your first wife was prettier. Mother never deceived herself about that. She used to say as she dusted the photo of your first wedding: 'La Xeta was the most beautiful girl in Balaguer.'

Teresa

1960

24 Ptrska Street
Prague

To my daughter Teresa,

The next year a friend of the family, came up to the house and said to me: 'We've got to get you married, young man.' She began flattering me: how hard working I was, what a good fellow, so bright and so on. I could make the choosiest girl in Balaguer happy, and she knew of someone who was crazy about me. Finally I asked indifferently: 'Who is it?' And she shouted: 'La Moreneta, the shepherd's daughter.' And that's when your mother came into my life.

I had never noticed La Moreneta. She was from a family seldom seen in the streets. I discovered that she had a house as well as a bit of land. I also discovered (later) that the whole plot had been hatched by my mother and that an interview with La Moreneta had already been arranged for the following Sunday. They brought her to the house all dressed up, with gold ear-rings and shoes with rows of buttons. We were married the next month.

Tomás

1968

Paris

Dear Father,

When my brother Pauet came to visit us in Prague he said to you: 'Mother really must have suffered with you.' You shrugged your shoulders and said nothing. I was struck by his accusation and by your response. Perhaps mother did suffer with a husband like you. I remember how the neighbours' wives used to tell her that she had trouble on her hands—with you always in some political mess. She smiled in her characteristic way and maintained that all men had to get mixed up in something: some gambled, some ran after women, some drank, others were layabouts; hers went in for politics. 'My husband is helping to make the social revolution,' she'd say. And when they asked her what that was she'd reply: 'It means giving bread to those who haven't any by taking it away from those who've got too much.' And it was in fact mother who carried the weight of that 'social revolution', in order that you could call yourself revolutionary. And she did it so well that we children all became revolutionaries.

I don't know whether *you* loved mother; I never saw you kiss her. 'Peasants don't kiss,' grandmother used to say. I never saw you at her side in the street. You never took her dancing or to the cinema or a show. She would never go to the cafés where you went, let alone the dives you'd frequent to have a good time with the girls. Pauet was probably right in his reproach but it made me sad. And when I saw how you shrugged your shoulders I felt a wave of compassion for you in your old age, an old age which suddenly seemed dreadful without mother, without her growing old beside you because she had died young.

Teresa

1961

24 Ptrska Street
Prague

To my daughter Teresa,

I need to explain how the nineteen men of Balaguer were killed, a crime now attributed to me according to the letter I received from the Spanish consul in Vienna when I applied for a passport. At dawn three lorry loads of '*milicianos*' arrived, armed with machine-guns and hand-grenades. They occupied the Post Office and the Town Hall where Dr Verdaguer and I were on guard—he as an independent Republican and I as representative of the Catalan Socialist Party. The *milicianos* were accompanied by three boys from the POUM [*Partido Obrero de unificación Marxista*, a militant communist faction] who declared, wild with excitement, that the fascists had just murdered one of their men on the road near Lérida. They wanted revenge. I knew one of the POUM members, and almost succeeded in convincing him that we couldn't take the simple line of 'an eye for an eye'. The others—spur-of-the-moment anarchists, drunk with dynamite—were in no mood to yield. One of them, the leader, holding a bomb in his hand as if it were an apple, shouted: 'We've come to search for bloody fascists and we're not going to leave with lily-white hands.' A member of the town council, a moderate, agreed, and went with them to the jail where the reactionaries of Balaguer and some friars from the convent of Santo Domingo and the Escolapios were awaiting trial. Dr Verdaguer and I tried to prevent what happened at the risk of our lives, but they accused us of being 'soft'. They were thirsting for fascist blood.

They removed nineteen prisoners from the jail and left them scattered on the road, a few paces apart, like sheaves of grain fallen from the carts during harvest.

When in 1957 I applied to the Spanish Consul in Vienna for a passport, I was told: 'Permission is refused because of your responsibility in the murder of . . .' and there followed the names of each of those nineteen men of Balaguer who died that morning: among them two cousins of mine, Franciscan friars.

Tomás

1968

Paris

Dear Father,

Our plane back to Paris was at eleven the next morning and so we took a walk around Prague. We headed for Staromesky Square, where we stopped at the shop of the locksmith Capek, the last Mohican of private enterprise in socialist Czechoslovakia. My brother wanted to photograph the old locksmith but as it happened the workshop was full of spotlights and TV technicians doing a report on him. Capek didn't like socialism because he didn't like progress. His shop is a heap of scrap-iron and old bits and pieces (I don't know whether this is still the case, since 21 August), but Capek is (was?) harmless. He was respected by the people of Prague as a relic of the past. I explained this to my brother and sister, and we all laughed, perhaps for the first time in Prague, the city in which you are buried.

We went into the Narodny Bank to change francs into Czech crowns. The clerk who dealt with us was a bit of a prehistoric figure too. He had a pearl tie-pin in his cheap, mass-produced tie, the kind that are sold in State department stores.

He had a yellow smile, the man with the pearl; yellow hands; yellow eyes. He spoke French and English. He noticed my brother's workman's hands at once and totally ignored him. My sister was wearing a fake fur coat and he treated her with great respect, as though he was attending a lady from the past; or perhaps the reason for this was her pounds sterling which are psychologically more impressive than the francs of 'La République Française'. I spoke to him in Czech and had no fur coat, only a plain, hand-knitted jersey. He replied to me in Italian. With his yellow hands he counted out the blue notes of the Czech Socialist Republic.

The man with the pearl and Capek, the locksmith: are these the counter-revolutionaries against which the armies and tanks of five countries have had to be sent? I must have the counter-revolutionary maggot in me too. I can honestly say that I've always felt a kind of pity for the man with the pearl and Capek, the locksmith. I don't consider them as enemies but as members of a class that has lost. Historically 'doomed' as you'd put it. But they are people.

Teresa

1961

24 Ptrska Street
Prague

To my daughter Teresa,

In the last year of the war I returned to Balaguer for my wife and two younger children but found no trace of them. Balaguer was in the grip of panic. There were people breaking into houses and shops, looting everything. The acquaintances I ran into barely listened when I asked them for news of my family, and by the next evening I gave up looking for them. I was fifty and in broken health. Wading across rivers and being out in all weathers had not been the best of remedies; my morale was very low.

Tomás

1968

Paris

Dear Father,

Each autumn the gardens of Libuse filled with dead leaves even as you tried to sweep them. The wind was strong in that part of Prague and whirled the leaves about so that you had to chase them with your spade. If it snowed the night before you found the leaves wet and dirty, soft and muddy, but easy to scoop up with the spade. You had a lovely view of the city. You could see the Vltava flowing round the island where sailing boats used to moor.

You suffered from asthma and it was difficult for you to get to the gardens every day, father, but you were never late. You believed that: 'A man's honour is in his work, whatever that work may be. It must be done well and conscientiously. Only after this have we the right to proclaim our beliefs. Never trust a communist who doesn't find pleasure in work.'

How you helped me during those days, father. I don't know what I would have done without you. I remember especially that day you broke the jar on the stairs when you were going to buy the midday beer. I was coming up the stairs with the little girl and, as I saw you, I shouted out: 'Oh father, such terrible news . . .' The little girl ran up the stairs with that laugh of children who can never really laugh or cry. Professor Novak had just given me the appalling and definitive diagnosis that she was mentally handicapped. I cried out: 'Oh father . . .'

The jar fell from your hands and you tried to push away the pieces with your foot in its open sandal. You sat down on the landing and covered your face with your rough peasant's hands. And those sobs of an old man gave me great comfort.

Things like that happen in people's lives. Their significance may not be apparent at the time. Years pass and then everything comes back. Even so, you can't talk of these things with other people. You must recall them in solitude or talk about them with the dead, as I'm doing now.

Teresa

1962

24 Ptrska Street
Prague

To my daughter Teresa,

I've seen many things in Czechoslovakia since that day in 1953 when my daughter hugged me at Prague Airport. I was present when Novotny took control of the country and the Party, or vice versa. I've seen socialism progressing like a crab and believe that the people to be blamed are the same kind who made us lose the war in Spain.

When I arrived there were meetings of the local electorate every Saturday in the beer-house round the corner. I never missed one. I'd be one of the first there and I'd ask for a beer and a couple of sausages and wait for the arrival of my neighbours and the deputy. I didn't understand the language, but I knew, and with such a feeling of satisfaction, that this really was democracy.

One day I persuaded my grandson, already a schoolboy, to come along with me. He translated a long discussion for me in the course of which everyone butted in, but quite amicably. The mothers were asking for a park so that when their children came out of school they'd have a nice place to wait until their mothers finished work. The deputy said there were no funds, but there and then, as they drank their beer and ate their sausages, they came up with a solution. Democracy and popular initiative can move mountains.

But now the meetings in the local beer-house have become more formal and less frequent. People shrug their shoulders when I ask them, in my Czech-Catalan, when the next one will be. There is something wrong with socialism in Czechoslovakia. I have the impression that the benefits of socialism, such as free education and medical care, are taken too much for granted, and if you tell people that many capitalist states have not solved these vital family problems, they listen to you without answering. I know old people with three pairs of glasses because they claim they need one pair for long distance, one for close-up and one just for seeing. What alarms me most is the state of mind of the working class. I couldn't care less about doctors, lawyers and pen-pushers, because they're not the real core of socialism.

Tomás

1970

Paris

Dear Father,

All of your pages have now finally arrived. I've followed your instructions and haven't added anything, though I have cut some bits that seemed cluttered. I suspect that there weren't really as many women in your life as I found in the pages, and I think I was right to cut out a couple of nuns and two or three insatiable housewives. I've left in the women I knew about and the ones I was sure had not been invented. My editing of these memories will seem arbitrary to you, and it is. Since we're speaking frankly I may as well tell you how greatly I disliked finding so many women in your biography. You devote ten pages to Soledad Fuentes from the time of her arrival in Balaguer, with that obnoxious family of hers. I can remember her going to mass with that huge cross around her neck, accompanied by her brother, a cretin. I used to make ladders in her stockings with gorse twigs. You devote pages and pages to mistresses and girl-friends.

For us there could be no woman in your life but our mother, and yet she is the only woman about whom you give no details. It seems as though your only real love was Agneta de los Xeta. The biggest photo in your room was of your first wedding and we grew up knowing—because mother told us—that the girl at our father's side was Agneta, who died giving birth to a stillborn child. Our *mother* was never a myth; we were never dazzled by *her*. She was simply the best mother in the world. There are things you don't know about her. We never had the chance to discuss them. But they can't be left out of your 'biography', because if you were able to accomplish 'great deeds'—as you write—it was precisely because there was a woman like our mother at your side.

You should have spoken about all this, and perhaps you should have kept quiet about other women. Am I asking you for the memories that I would have liked? Perhaps I am. Would they have been false? Maybe they would. No one has ever written a complete account of their life. Malraux has written that *'un homme c'est un petit tas de secrets.'* I wouldn't go that far; but in writing one's memories one's bound to have a bias, and it's very clear that you had yours.

Teresa

1970

Paris

Dear Father,

I was in Barcelona for a wedding. My five-day visit, spent among neighbours and acquaintances, all of 'progressive' opinions, was filled with stormy discussions. They considered me a traitor to my past and to your memory, father. The image they have of you is that of the true revolutionary, a consistent internationalist, intransigent against the class enemy. They'd have liked to be like you themselves, but life, inexorable, bloody life,

103

has turned them into bosses and owners of houses and of land—
but each one of them is still one of us; oh yes, very much so, with
ideals untouched. I wanted to tell them to go to hell, but I didn't. I
was affected by what they said, and finding myself alone among
that legion of the faithful, I didn't think it wise to defend what I
believe in.

I no longer weep. I no longer send SOS's to my dead father as I
did two years ago, entreating him to invent a quotation from Lenin
to help me out of the mass of contradictions I found myself in. I'm
writing to you today not with a lump in my throat but with a sense
of dry, cold impotence, a state of mind that can easily topple into
cynicism. And I don't want that to happen. How can you fight
while stalling? I don't yet know but I shall have to learn.

Teresa

Translated from the Spanish by Diana Thorold

MARY MCCARTHY
FELLOW WORKERS

I t was 1936, and there I was, Mary Johnsrud, marching down lower Broadway in a May Day parade, chanting at the crowds watching on the sidewalk: 'FELLOW WORKERS, join our RANKS!' Nobody, I think, joined us; they just watched. We were having fun; beside me marched a tall, fair young man, former correspondent of the Paris *Herald*, who looked like Fred MacMurray. His name was John Porter. Johnsrud was on the road with Maxwell Anderson's *Winterset*, playing his Broadway role of the blind man. I had been out of college and married to him nearly three years.

Opposite: Communist Party May Day parade, New York, 1930.

Mary McCarthy

Since 1 October 1933, Johnsrud, known as 'John', and I had been living in New York in a one-room apartment at Two Beekman Place, a new building opposite One Beekman Place, where Ailsa Mellon Bruce and Blanchette Hooker Rockefeller lived. Most months we could not pay the rent. It was a pretty apartment, painted apricot with white trim; it had casement windows and Venetian blinds (a new thing then), a kitchen with a good stove, a 'breakfast alcove', and a dressing-room with bath besides a little front hall and the main room. Good closet space. Nice elevator boys and a doorman. Fortunately the man at Albert B. Ashforth, the building agent, had faith in John, and fortunately also the utilities were included in the rather high rent. The telephone company, being a 'soulless corporation', unlike dear Albert B. Ashforth, kept threatening to shut the phone off, but gas and electricity would keep on being supplied to us unless and until we were evicted.

If we *were* evicted and the furniture put out on the street (which did not happen in good neighbourhoods anyway), it would not be our own. We were living with my Miss Sandison's sister's furniture, Miss Sandison having been my Vassar Professor of English. We owned not a stick ourselves except a handsome card table with a cherrywood frame and legs and a blue suede top, which someone (probably Miss Sandison herself) had given us for a wedding-present. When we moved into Beekman Place, the Howlands (Lois Sandison, who taught Latin at Chapin) let us have their Hepplewhite-style chairs and the springs and mattresses of their twin beds, which we had mounted on pegs that we painted bright red and which we set up in the shape of an 'L' with the heads together—you couldn't have beds that looked like bedroom beds in a living-room, as our one room was supposed to be. Instead of spreads, we had covers made of dark brown sateen (Nathalie Swann's idea), and at the joint of the 'L', where our two heads converged, we put a small square carved oak table, Lois Sandison Howland's, too, with a white Chinese crack table-lamp that we had found at Macy's.

On the walls we had Van Gogh's red-lipped *Postmaster* (John's guardian spirit) from the Hermitage and Harry Sternberg's drawing of John looking like Lenin. Then there were Elizabeth

Photo (preceding pages): Popperfoto

Bishop's wedding-present, bought in Paris—a coloured print, framed in white, rather surreal, called *Geometry*, by Jean Hugo, great-grandson of the author—and my Vassar friend Frani's wedding-present—a black-framed, seventeenth-century English broadside, on 'The Earl of Essex Who cut his own Throat in the Tower'—not Elizabeth's Essex, brother to Penelope Devereux, but a later one, no longer of the Devereux family. Probably the apartment had built-in bookcases, which (already!) held the 1911 *Britannica*. I am sure of that because I wrote a fanciful piece (turned down by the *New Yorker*) called 'FRA to GIB'. I don't know where that *Britannica*, the first of its line in my life, came from or where it went to; maybe it was Mrs Howland's. On the floor, I think, were two oriental rugs, hers, too, obviously. In two white *cachepôts* (Macy's) we had English ivy trailing.

To reassure a reader wondering about our moral fibre and ignorant of those Depression years, I should say that Mr and Mrs Howland (I could never call them 'Lois and 'Harold') kindly made us feel that we were doing them a service by 'storing' their things while they, to economize, lived at the National Arts Club on Gramercy Park, Mr Howland being out of a job. We had bought ourselves a tall, 'modernistic' Russel Wright cocktail-shaker made of aluminium with a wood top, a chromium hors-d'oeuvres tray with glass dishes (using industrial materials was the idea), and six silver old-fashioned spoons with a simulated cherry at one end and the bottom of the spoon flat, for crushing sugar and Angostura; somewhere I still have these and people who come upon them always wonder what they are.

Late one morning, but before we had got the beds made, 'Mrs Langdon Mitchell' was announced over the house-phone, and the widow of the famous (now forgotten) playwright sailed in to pay a formal call, which lasted precisely the ordained fifteen minutes although we were in our night clothes and she, white-haired, hatted and gloved, sat on a Hepplewhite chair facing our tumbled sheets. We must have met this old lady at one of Mrs Aldrich's temperance lunches in the house on Riverside Drive, where the conversation was wont to hover over 'dear Beatrice and Sidney (Webb)' and Bis Meyer, my class-mate, daughter of Eugene Meyer of the Federal Reserve Bank, was described as 'a beautiful Eurasian', a gracious way our hostess had found of saying Jewish. Mr Aldrich had been the music critic of the *New York Times*. John and I had gone up to Rokeyby, the Aldriches' country house, for Maddie Aldrich's wedding to Christopher Rand, a Yale classic major and an Emmet on his mother's side whom Maddie had met, hunting, on weekends. At the wedding, Maddie's cousin Chanler Chapman (*A Bad Boy at a Good School*, son of John Jay Chapman and model, in due course, for Bellow's *Henderson the Rain King*) had spiked Mrs Aldrich's awful grape-juice 'libation' and got some of the ushers drunk. Now the couple had an all-blue apartment with a Judas peep-hole in the door, Chris had a job with Luce on *Fortune*, and Maddie had started a business called 'Dog Walk'.

I think about the dances at Webster Hall, organized by the Communist Party. That was where I had met John Porter (I had better start calling him 'Porter', so as not to mix him up with 'John'), who had been brought by Eunice Clark, the class-mate who had edited the Vassar *Miscellany News*. Eunice was always trendy, and I guess we were all what was later called 'swingers'; Webster Hall was an 'in' thing to do for Ivy League New Yorkers—a sort of downtown slumming; our uptown slumming was done at the Savoy Ballroom in Harlem, usually on Friday nights. Maybe real Communists steered clear of Webster Hall, just as ordinary black people did not go to the Savoy on those Friday nights when so many white people came.

I remember one Webster Hall evening—was it the Porter time?—when John and I had brought Alan Lauchheimer (Barth) with us and he found some class-mates from Yale there, in particular one called Bill Mangold who would soon be doing PR for medical aid to the Spanish Loyalists—a Stalinist front—and with whom I would later have an affair. At Webster Hall, too, we met the very 'in' couple, Tony Williams, a gentleman gentlemen's tailor (see 'Dog Walk' and the Don Budge-Wood laundry firm) who had married Peggy LeBoutiller (Best's); they knew Eunice Clark and her husband, Selden Rodman, brother of Nancy Rodman, Dwight Macdonald's wife.

Selden and Alfred Bingham (son of Senator Bingham of Connecticut) were editors of *Common Sense*, a Lafolletteish magazine they had started after Yale. 'Alf' was married to Sylvia Knox, whose brother Sam was married to Kay McLean from Vassar; both were trainees at Macy's. At a party at the Knoxes' I met Harold Loeb, the technocrat and former editor of *Broom* and a character in *The Sun Also Rises* (related also to Loeb of Loeb and Leopold, murderers). Leaning back on a couch while talking to him about Technocracy and having had too much to drink, I lost my balance in the midst of a wild gesture and tipped over on to a sizzling steam radiator. As he did not have the presence of mind to pull me up, I bear the scars on the back of my neck to this day.

Before that, Selden, in black tie, had led a walk-out of diners in support of a waiters' strike at the Waldorf, which Johnsrud and I joined, also in evening dress—Eunice was wearing a tiara. At another table Dorothy Parker and Alexander Woollcott and Heywood Broun got up to walk out, too. The Waldorf dicks chased Selden out of the Rose Room and into the basement, where they tried to beat him up. Then he was taken to be charged at the East 51st Street police station while some of us waited outside to pay his bail and bring him back home to Eunice. It was all in the papers the next day, though Johnsrud and I were too unknown to be in the story. The reader will find some of it, including Eunice's tiara and a pair of long white kid gloves in, in chapters six and seven of *The Group*. It was the only time I saw Dorothy Parker close up, and I was disappointed by her dumpy appearance. Today television talk-shows would have prepared me.

At Selden and Eunice's apartment—in a watermelon-pink house on East 49th Street—in the course of a summer party in the little backyard, I met John Strachey, then in his Marxist phase (*The Coming Struggle for Power*) and married to Esther Murphy (Mark Cross, and sister of Gerald Murphy, the original of Dick Diver in *Tender is the Night*); I was shocked when he went to the toilet to pee—they were serving beer—and left the door open, continuing a conversation while he unbuttoned his fly and let go with a jet of urine. English manners? I wondered. Or was it the English left?

Mary McCarthy

I was having class-war problems with the *New Republic*. The pipe-smoking Malcolm Cowley—'Bunny' (Edmund) Wilson's successor as literary editor—though a faithful fellow-traveller, was too taciturn usually to show his hand. After the first book he had given me to review, when I was still in college, he almost never gave me another but let me come week after week to the house on West 21st Street that was the *New Republic*'s office then—quite a ride for me on the Ninth Avenue El. Wednesday was Cowley's 'day' for receiving reviewers; after a good hour spent eyeing each other in the reception room, one by one we mounted to Cowley's office, where shelves of books for review were ranged behind the desk, and there again we waited while he wriggled his eyebrows and silently puffed at his pipe as though trying to make up his mind. Sometimes, perhaps to break the monotony, he would pass me on to his young assistant, Robert Cantwell, who had a little office down the hall. Cantwell was a Communist, a real member, I guess, but unlike Cowley, he was nice. He was fair and slight, with a somewhat rabbity appearance, and he, too, came from the Pacific Northwest, which gave us something to talk about. 'Cantwell tells me the story of his life,' I wrote to my friend Frani in December 1933. In 1931, he had published a novel, *Laugh and Lie Down*, and in 1934 he would publish a second, *The Land of Plenty*. Both were about Puget Sound and were described to me later by a Marxist critic as 'Jamesian'—he counted as the only proletarian novelist with a literary style. I had not read him then; nor had I read Cowley's *Blue Juniata* or *Exile's Return*, but with Cantwell that did not matter. After the *New Republic*, he went to work for *Time* and moved to the right, like Whittaker Chambers, who may well have been his friend. The other day someone wrote me that Lillian Hellman tried to stage a walk-out from Kenneth Fearing's funeral service because Cantwell was one of the speakers. Can you imagine? Yes. Now he is dead himself. I should have liked to thank him for his interesting book, *The Hidden Northwest*, which led me to Washington Irving's *Astoria*—a happy discovery. I learn from my 1978–79 *Who's Who* (he was still living then) that he was named Robert Emmett Cantwell. A misnomer, typically North-western, for Robert Emmet, the Irish patriot? A spelling error by *Who's Who*? Or just no connection?

112

Cowley had another cohort, very different, by the name of Otis Ferguson, a real proletarian who had been a sailor in the Merchant Marine. 'Oat' was not in the book department; he wrote movie reviews. But he carried great weight with Cowley, though he may not have been a Marxist—he was more of a free-ranging literary bully without organizational ties. I had a queer time with him one evening when John and I went to look him up at his place on Cornelia Street, the deepest in the Village I had yet been. At our ring he came downstairs but, instead of asking us up to his place, he led us out to a bar for a drink, which seemed unfriendly, as he had given me his address and told me to drop by. I am not sure whether it was John or me that made him edgy or the pair of us—*notre couple*, as the French say. Perhaps he and John argued about films—John had worked in Hollywood, after all. Or could it have been simply that we had come down from Beekman Place? Anyway whatever happened that evening and whatever caused it cannot have been the reason for my sudden fall from favour at the *New Republic*. No.

It was a book: *I Went to Pit College*, by Lauren Gilfillan, a Smith girl who had spent a year working in a coal-mine—one of the years when I had been at Vassar. Cowley must have thought that here at last was a book I was qualified to review, by having had the contrary experience. The book was causing a stir, and Cowley, as he handed it over to me, benignly, let me understand that he was *giving me my chance*. I sensed a reservation on his part, as though he were cautioning me not to let the book down. He was allowing me plenty of space, to do a serious review, not another 300-word bit. And with my name, I dared hope, on the cover. I got the message: I was supposed to like the book. For the first time, and the last, I wrote to order. It would have been nice if I could have warmed to the task. But the best I could do was to try to see what people like Cowley saw in the book. With the result, of course, that I wrote a lifeless review, full of simulated praise. In short a cowardly review. Re-reading it now, for the first time, in more than fifty years, I am amazed at how convincing I sound. In my last sentence I speak of a 'terrific reality'.

But then came the blow. Cowley had second thoughts about the book. Whether the Party line had changed on it or for some other reason he now decided that it was overrated. I cannot remember whether he tried to get me to rewrite my review. I think he did but, if so, he was unsatisfied. In any case, he printed my laudatory piece and followed it with *a correction*. The correction was signed only with initials: O.C.F. 'Oat', of course. In fact it must have been he who changed Cowley's mind. As a blue-collar reader, he had looked over the Smith girl's book—or read my review of it—and responded with disgust. Which he expressed to Cowley. And, 'Write that,' said Cowley. Whereupon 'Oat' did. A 300-word snarl, merited or unmerited—who knows? I cannot really blame 'Oat' for the effect of those jeers on my feelings. Cowley would hardly have told him that he had virtually *ordered* a favourable review.

But had he? Trying to be fair to him, I asked myself now whether I could have misread the signals: could he have been telling me to pan the book? I do not think so. But either way the lack of openness was wrong. And it was a mean trick to play on a beginner; when my review came out, in May 1934, I was not yet twenty-two. I agree that a lot of the fault was mine: I should have written my real opinion, regardless of what he wanted. But abuse of power is worse than girlish weakness, and Cowley was a great abuser of power, as he proved over and over in his long 'affair' with Stalinism: for this, see under 'Cowley' in *Letters on Literature and Politics* by Edmund Wilson, edited by Elena Wilson. But it cannot have been all Stalinism; he must have taken a personal dislike to me. I leave it to the reader to decide between us.

For Selden Rodman at *Common Sense*, I had written a review (very favourable) of *The Young Manhood of Studs Lonigan*, the second volume of the Studs Lonigan trilogy. Farrell called or wrote to thank me. All we had in common was being Irish, middle-western, ex-Catholic and liking baseball (and I was only half-midwestern and half-Irish), but Farrell, gregarious and hospitable, took to me anyway, and when John was on the road with *Winterset*, I went to gatherings at his place, though I felt like a complete outsider. Farrell was married to or lived with an actress (Hortense Alden; I had seen her in *Grand Hotel*), but there was nobody from the theatre at those evenings. Now, half a century later, I know that she had had an affair with Clifford Odets and I wonder what Farrell made of that, which may have happened before his time.

In the apartment Farrell and Hortense shared on Lexington Avenue, the guests were all intellectuals, of a kind unfamiliar to me. I could hardly understand them as they ranted and shouted at each other. What I was witnessing was the break-up of the Party's virtual monopoly on the thought of the left. Among the writers who had been converted to Marxism by the Depression, Farrell was one of the first to free himself. The thing that was happening in that room, around the drinks table, was important and eventful. An orthodoxy was cracking, like ice-floes on the Volga. But I was not in a position to grasp this, being still, so to speak, pre-Stalinist in my politics, while the intellectuals I heard debating were on the verge of post-Stalinism—a dangerous slope. Out of the shouting and the general blur, only two figures emerge: Rahv and Phillips. Farrell made a point of introducing them, and I knew who they were—the editors of *Partisan Review*. As the popular song said, my future just passed.

It was odd, actually, that I knew of the magazine; it must have had a very small circulation. But a couple who ran a stationery store on First Avenue, around the corner from our apartment, had recommended it to me, knowing that I wrote for the *Nation*. They were Party members, surely—of the type of Julius and Ethel Rosenberg, though the wife was much prettier than Ethel. And *Partisan Review* was a Party publication, the organ of the John Reed Club. But I had no inkling of that then; skill in recognizing Communists came to me much later. When the pair of stationers showed me an early issue of the magazine, the husband running from behind the counter to fetch it, the wife proudly watching as I turned the pages, I found that it was over my head. It was devoted to an onslaught on the American Humanists—Stuart Sherman and Paul Elmer More—with a few rancorous side-swipes at the Southern Agrarians—Tate and Ransom, the group called the Fugitive Poets. I do not remember any fiction or poetry, only long, densely written articles in a language that might as well have been Russian. I was distantly familiar with the Humanists, having read about them in the *Bookman*, but these Agrarians were a mystery to me, and *PR*'s crushing brief against them left me bewildered. As for the dreary Humanists, I was surprised that they needed so much attacking. In fact Rahv and Phillips and their colleagues were beating a dead horse there.

Nevertheless, to please the stationers, with whom we were friendly, I kept buying the magazine and trying my best to read it. There is a sad little sequel to my introduction to *Partisan Review*. It ceased publication when the Party cut off funds from the John Reed Clubs (it was announced that they would be replaced by an American Writers Congress); this may have already happened when I met the editors at Farrell's. And when *Partisan Review* resumed, still edited by Rahv and Phillips but without Jack Conroy *et al* on the mast-head, it had changed colour. Dwight Macdonald and Fred Dupee and I and George L. K. Morris, our backer, were on the new editorial board, and *PR* was now anti-Stalinist. Some time later, maybe when my first book was published, out of the blue came a shrill letter, many times forwarded, from the Mitchell Stationers accusing me of running out on a bill John and I owed them. I cannot remember what I did about it, if anything.

In our Beekman Place apartment, besides *Partisan Review*, I was trying to read *Ulysses*. John in the breakfast nook was typing his play *University* (about his father and never produced), and I was writing book reviews. Every year I started *Ulysses*, but I could not get beyond the first chapter—'stately, plump Buck Mulligan'—page forty-seven, I think it was. Then one day, long after, in a different apartment, with a different man (which?), I found myself on page forty-eight and never looked back. This happened with many of us: *Ulysses* gradually—but with an effect of suddenness—became accessible. It was because in the interim we had been reading diluted Joyce in writers like Faulkner and so had got used to his ways, at second remove. During the modernist crisis this was happening in all the arts; imitators and borrowers taught the 'reading' of an artist at first thought to be beyond the public power of comprehension. In the visual arts, techniques of mass reproduction—imitation on a wide scale—had the same function. Thanks to reproduction, the public got used to faces with two noses or an eye in the middle of the forehead, just as a bit earlier the 'funny' colours of the Fauves stopped looking funny except to a few.

When the first Moscow trial took place and Zinoviev and Kamenev were executed in August 1936 (and the Spanish Civil War began), I did not know about it, as I was in Reno. Shortly after that May Day parade, I had told John, who was back from playing *Winterset* on the road. I said I was in love with John Porter and wanted to marry him. This was in Central Park while we watched some ducks swimming, as described in 'Cruel and Barbarous Treatment'. Except for that detail, there is not much resemblance between the reality and the story I wrote two years later—the first I ever published. When I wrote that story (which became the opening chapter of *The Company She Keeps*), I was trying, I think, to give some form to what had happened between John, John Porter and me, in other words, to explain it to myself. But I do not see that I was really like the nameless heroine, and the two men are shadows, deliberately so. I know for a fact that when I wrote that piece I was feeling the effects of reading a lot of Henry James, yet today I cannot find James there either—no more than the living triangle of John, John Porter and me.

John Porter was tall, weak, good-looking, a good dancer; his favourite writer was Remy de Gourmont, and he had an allergy to eggs in any form. He went to Williams (I still have his Psi U pin) and was the only son of elderly parents. When I met him, he had been out of work for some time and lived by collecting rents on Brooklyn and Harlem real estate for his mother; the family, de-gentrifying, occupied the last 'white' house in Harlem, on East 122nd Street, and owned the beautiful old silver communion cup from Trinity Church in Brooklyn; it must have been given to an ancestor as the last vestryman. After the Paris *Herald* and Agence Havas, John had worked in Sweden for the Women's International League for Peace and Freedom, but since then had been unable to connect with a job. Collecting rents on the wretched tenements still owned by his parents was his sole recourse, and most of the poor blacks who lived in them dodged him as best they could, having no earnings either. The Porters were very close with the little they had; they neither drank nor smoked and disapproved of anybody who did. The old father, who had once been an assemblyman in Albany, was deaf and inattentive, and John hid his real life from his mother.

He was in love with me or thought he was; my energy must have made an appeal to him—he probably hoped it would be catching. Despite his unemployment, dour mother, rent-collecting, he was gay and full of charm. He was fond of making love and giving pleasure. By the time John came back from the road, Porter and I had a future planned. Together with a journalist friend who had a car, he was going to write a travel book on Mexico. Mexico was very much 'in' then among sophisticated people, especially as Europe, what with Hitler and the fall of the dollar, was looking more and more forbidding. Hence John and his co-author had readily found a publisher to advance 500 dollars on a book contract with royalties.

It may be that Porter already had the idea of the Mexican book at the time he met me and merely needed the thought of marriage to spur him on. In any case, I fitted into the picture. After Reno, where my grandfather was getting me the best law firm to file for divorce, Porter would wait while I visited my grandparents in Seattle, and then the three of us would start out from New York in the friend's small car. It would be an adventure.

And Johnsrud? He took it hard, much harder than I had been prepared for. I felt badly for him; in fact I was torn. The worst was that, when it came down to it, I did not know why I was leaving him. I still had love of some sort left for him, and seeing him suffer made me know it. Out of our quarrelling, we had invented an evil, spooky character called 'Hohnsrud' (from a misaddressed package) who accounted for whatever went wrong. Our relations in bed, on my side, were unsatisfactory, and infidelity had shown me that with other men that was not so. It was as though something about John, our history together, made me impotent, if that can be said of women. I had no trouble even with an earnest little actor in Adler elevated shoes. Yet I doubt that sex was really the force that was propelling me; had we stayed together I might well have outgrown whatever the inhibition was. I was still immensely impressed by him and considered myself his inferior. Hence it stupefied me, shortly after our break-up, to hear Frani say, by way of explanation: 'Well, your being so brilliant must have been difficult for him!'

It is a mystery. No psychoanalyst ever offered a clue, except to tell me that I felt compelled to leave the men I loved because my parents had left *me*. Possibly. What I sensed myself was inexorability, the *moirae* at work, independently of my will, of my likes or dislikes. A sweet, light-hearted love affair, all laughter and blown kisses, like Porter himself, had turned leaden with pointless consequence. Looking back, I am sorry for poor Porter, that he had to be the instrument fated to separate me from John. And for him it *was* a doom, which took him in charge, like the young Oedipus meeting the stranger, Laius, at the crossroads; I wonder whether he may not have felt it himself as he finally set out for Mexico, where he would die of a fever after over-staying his visa and going to jail. All alone in a stable or primitive guest quarter belonging to a woman who had been keeping him and then got tired of it.

Meanwhile, though, before I left for Reno, Porter and I went out for a few days to Watermill, Long Island, where his parents still owned a mouldy summer bungalow in the tall grass high up over the sea. With us was a little Communist organizer by the name of Sam Craig. I have told the story of that in the piece called 'My Confession' in *On the Contrary*. The gist of it is that the Party was sending him to California in a car some sympathizer had donated. But Sam did not know how to drive. So he had asked Porter, a long-time friend, to take the car and give him driving lessons on the lonely back roads around Watermill. Sam was a slow learner, to the point of tempting us to despair for him. On the beach, all that week the red danger flags of the Coast Guard were out, and we swam only once in the rough water. In the evenings, over drinks in the mouldy old house lit by oil lamps, Sam was trying to convert me to communism. To my many criticisms of the Party, he had a single answer: I should join the Party and work from the inside to reform it. This was a variant on 'boring from within', the new tactic that corresponded with the new line; the expression seems to have been first used in 1936. Evidently Sam was thinking of termite work to be done on the Party itself, rather than on some capitalist institution. Very original on his part, and he nearly convinced me.

In the end, I said I would think it over. Sam passed his driving test and went off by himself in the car, heading west. As I wrote in 'My Confession', I ask myself now whether this wasn't the old car that figured in the Hiss case—the car Alger gave to the Party. I never learned what happened to Sam. He may have perished in the desert or gone to work recruiting among the Okies or on the waterfront. And here is the eerie thing about the Porter chain of events: everyone concerned with him disappeared. First, Sam; next the man named Weston, Porter's collaborator on the Mexican guidebook, who vanished from their hotel room in Washington after drinks one night at the National Press Club, leaving his typewriter and all his effects behind.

Porter searched for a week, enlisting police help; they canvased the Potomac, the jails, the docks, the hospitals, talked to those who had last seen him. The best conclusion was that he had been shanghaied. By a Soviet vessel? Or that he had had some reason to want to disappear. But without his typewriter? A journalist does not do that. He was never found.

Meanwhile I, too, had dropped out of the picture. I was in New York, at the Lafayette Hotel and concurring by telephone with the decision Porter came to: to go on to Mexico without Weston and get the book started, while he still had the car and half the advance. Of course I had qualms. Even though he had taken it with good grace when, on my return from Reno and Seattle, I had got cold feet about the Mexican trip. I forget what reason I gave. The fact was, I had lost my feeling for him. But I let him think I might join him once he had 'prepared the way.' From Washington he wrote or telephoned every day; after he left, I wrote, too, day after day, addressing my letters to Laredo, general delivery. I never heard from him again.

Late that fall, a crude-looking package from an unknown sender arrived in the little apartment I had taken on Gay Street in the Village. Having joined the Committee for the Defense of Leon Trotsky, whose members were getting a certain number of anonymous phone calls—Sidney Hook, we heard, looked under the bed every night before retiring—I was afraid to open the thing.

As far as I could make out from the scrawled handwriting, it came from Laredo, on the Mexican border; conceivably there was a connection with Trotsky and his murderous enemies in Coyoacan. I am ashamed to say that I asked Johnsrud if he would come over and be with me while I opened it. He did—first we listened, to be sure we could not hear anything ticking—but inside all we found was a quite hideous pony-skin throw lined with the cheapest, sleaziest sky-blue rayon, totally unlike Porter, who had a gift for present-giving. I had already ruled out any likelihood that the crudely wrapped package had anything to do with him, even though Laredo had been on his way. The sleazy throw confirmed this. On Johnsrud's advice probably, I wrote or wired the sender. In reply, I got a telegram: 'PACKAGE COMES FROM JOHN PORTER MEXICO.'

That was all. At some point that autumn his mother wrote me, demanding that I pay her for the telephone calls he made to me in Seattle. I refused. Next, his parents wanted to know, perhaps through a third party, whether I had heard from him at Christmas—they had not. But my memory here is hazy. And I cannot remember when I finally learned of his death. It was more than a year later, and it seems to me that it came to me in two different versions, from different sources. Certainly the second was from Marshall Best, a Viking Press editor who lived at Two Beekman Place and served special meatballs baked in salt. He was a devoted friend of Porter's and, if I may say it, quite a devoted Stalinist sympathizer. By now, naturally, with the Trotsky Defense Committee, he disliked me on political grounds. It may have given him some satisfaction to tell me a piece of news that was not only painful but reflected poorly on me. As though I were the principal cause of Porter's death. And perhaps, in truth, I was. His mother must have thought so.

If it had not been for me, he would never have *been* in Mexico. He would still be collecting rents for his parents. And, if I had gone along with him, instead of copping out, I would *never* have let him overstay his visa, which had caused him to land in prison, which caused him to contract diphtheria or typhus or whatever it was that killed him when, on his release, the woman he had been living with let him come back and stay in her stables.

Well. As an English writer said to me, quoting Orwell, an autobiography that does not tell something bad about the author cannot be any good.

I am not sure why I lost my feeling for Porter. At the time I thought it was his letters—wet, stereotyped, sentimental—that had killed my love. The deflation was already beginning, obviously, when I met the man in the Brooks Brothers shirt on the train that was taking me west. The letters and phone calls completed the process. Whatever it was, I now realize that I positively disliked that Fred MacMurray look-alike when I saw him gazing fondly down at me when he met me on my return. The distaste was physical as well as intellectual. I could not stand him. He had become an embarrassment, having served his purpose, which I suppose was to dissolve my marriage. I was appalled, for him and for myself.

Did he notice that I had changed? Nothing was ever said, and I tried to hide it. '*Succès*?' '*Succès fou!*' had been our magic formula after love-making, and '*Succès fou!*' I went on duly repeating, I imagine. I was telling myself that it was only a few days; in a few days he would have left. Such cowardice was very bad of me. If I had had the courage to tell him, he might not have started out without me. Yet I am not sure. Would my having 'the heart' to tell him have made the difference? Probably the truth was that Porter *had* to go to Mexico; his bridges were burned. That applied to all three of us. Nothing could return to the *status quo ante*. John and I had left Two Beekman Place behind, to the tender mercies of Albert B. Ashforth, who painted our pretty apricot walls another colour, I suppose. The Howlands' furniture had been passed on to a friend of Alan Barth's named Lois Brown. A trunk with my letters and papers in it went to storage, never to be reclaimed. Johnsrud had moved to the Village. While waiting for my grandfather to fix things up with Thatcher & Woodburn in Reno, I had stayed with Nathalie Swan in her parents' Georgian house in the East 80s. No, nothing could go back to what it had been.

Old Clara, my Harlem maid, returned to her funeral-parlour business—she was proud of having buried a fighter named Tiger Flowers. I never ate her smothered chicken again. Poor 'Hohnsrud' of course had died.

Moreover, Porter was sensitive—think of his allergies. He must have heard the difference on the telephone while I was still in Seattle; I am a fairly transparent person. And if he guessed my changed feelings, he kept it strictly to himself. The question I should ask myself is not did he know but how *soon* did he know? It is a rather shaking thought.

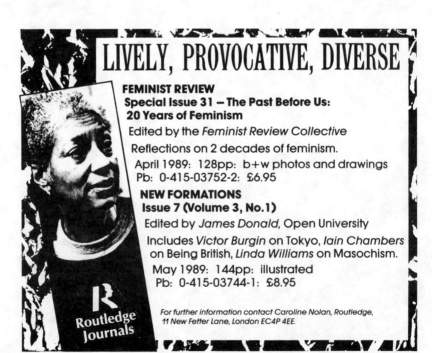

ADAM MARS-JONES
BABY CLUTCH

136361

Department of Transport Approved Driving Instructor

Valid until last day of **AUG 1991**

D 0355404

EXPIRES

3 12 89

12 89

Ford

DAGENHAM
MOTORS

XXX **Triplex**
laminated

The half-dozen Walkmans that used to live on this ward, bought by a charity for the use of the patients, were walked off with in a matter of days. The next batch, if the charity decides to replace them, will have to be chained down, I expect, like books in a medieval library.

At least the television in my lover's room has a remote control; that's something. There used to be a remote for every room on the ward, but one or two have also gone walkies. Replacing them isn't a high medical priority, though perhaps it should be. Life on this ward can seem like one big game of musical chairs, as if death, being spoiled for choice, will come by preference to the person with no flowers by the bed, with no yoghurts stashed away in the communal fridge, the person whose TV has no remote control.

A television looms larger in a hospital room than it could ever do in someone's home. There are so few excuses not to watch it: visitors, coma. Once I came in and was shocked to see a nurse comforting my lover. She was bending over him with a tenderness that displaced me. My lover was sobbing and saying, '*Poor Damon*'; it was a while before he could make himself understood. The nurse wasn't amused when she found out Damon was a young man on *Brookside* who'd just been killed.

She'd have been even less amused if she'd known it was the first episode of *Brookside* my lover had ever watched, so he hadn't seen poor Damon alive. But I suppose it was the mother's grief having no actual content for him that let him share it so fully.

There's another television in the day-room, which even has a video recorder and a little shelf of tapes. The day-room also contains an eccentric library, *Ring of Bright Water* rubbing spines with a guide to non-nuclear defence and a fair selection of periodicals. My lover and I find ourselves listing the self-descriptions we find least beguiling in the small ads of the gay press.

'Antibody-negative,' is his first contribution. He resents the assumption that good health is as intrinsic to some people as blue eyes are to others, or the condition, so common on these pages, of being 'considered attractive'.

It's my turn. 'Straight-appearing.'

'Healthy,' is second on my lover's list.

'Discreet.' What kind of boast is that, after all?

'Healthy.' My lover can't seem to get over this little preoccupation of his, so I shut myself up, without even mentioning *non-camp, looks younger, genuine* or *first-time advertiser.*

Deep down I'm pleased by the silliness of the small ads, pleased to find any evidence that there are still trivial sides to gay life. More than anything, I want there to be disco bunnies out there somewhere, still. But I expect even the disco bunnies are stoic philosophers these days, if only in their free time. What used to be the verdict on men who loved men—something about being locked in the nursery, wasn't it? There's nothing like being locked in a hospice to make the nursery look good.

We are having a respite between waves of my lover's visitors. Less than half-joking, I suggest that one of the nurses on the ward should function as a secretary, to make appointments and space the visitors out, to avoid these log-jams of well-wishers. I resent the brutal etiquette of hospital visiting, which means that a new visitor tapping hesitantly at the porthole instantly shuts down our intimacy. I try to be tactful, do some shopping in the area or talk to one of the other patients, but I doubt if I manage to be nice about it. Making myself scarce only encourages the other visitors to stay, to cling like leeches. I find the whole business of dealing with the visitors exhausting, and I'm not even ill.

Gently, taking care not to scare off his good fortune, my lover tells me that he is the only patient now on the ward who would benefit from a secretarial service like the one I am proposing. The other inmates have, at the most, two guests at a time. The difference may be one of character (my lover is agreed to be lovable); it may also turn out that the other patients have come back here so many times they have lost the ability to reassure their visitors, after which point the visits tend to dry up.

This is my lover's first major stay in hospital. Transfusions for anaemia don't count, even when he is there overnight. Everybody I come across refers to transfusions in the cheeriest possible terms ('just in for a top-up, are you?' is the standard phrase) though everybody also knows that transfusions can't go on for ever. That's an example of something I've been noticing recently, of how easy it is for people to rise above the fates of third parties.

I'm generally impatient with the visitors, but I make exceptions. I'm always glad to see Armchair, for instance. My lover knows so many Davids and so many Peters he gives them nicknames to tell them apart. Armchair is a Peter; other Peters are Poodle and Ragamuffin.

Armchair is, as advertised, reassuring and cosy, all the more comfortable for having one or two springs broken. Armchair is a fine piece of supportive furniture. When he phones the hospital to leave a message, he doesn't bother any more with his proper name; he just says Armchair. A nurse will come into the room and say, 'Someone called Armchair asks if it's all right to visit,' or, 'Armchair sends his love,' with a faint gathering of the eyebrows, until she's used to these messages.

Armchair is actually, in his way, my lover's deputy lover, or I suppose I mean my deputy. They met a month or two ago, while I was away, and they've slept together once or twice, but it's clear enough that Armchair would like More. It isn't a physical thing between them, exactly—my lover isn't awash with libido at the moment—but Armchair would like my lover to spend nights with him on a more permanent basis. Armchair would like to be a regular fixture at bedtime.

I wouldn't mind. It's my lover who's withdrawn a bit. But Armchair assumes I'm the problem and seems to think he's taking a huge risk by putting his hand on my lover's leg. My lover's arms are sore from the VenFlow, the little porthole the doctors keep open there, and his legs have taken over from them as the major pattable and squeezable parts. My lover's blood, beneath the porthole, is—as we know—full of intercepted messages of healing and distress.

Armchair looks at me with a colossal reproach. But can he really want to sit where I sit? Where I sit is sometimes behind my lover on the bed, wedging him as best I can during a retching fit, so that he is cushioned against the pain of his pleurisy. I hold on to his shoulders, which offer a reasonable guarantee of not hurting him. My medical encyclopaedia tells me that the pleura are 'richly supplied with pain fibres.' My lover has worked this out all by himself.

My lover threatens to give Armchair the yo-heave-ho. I tell him to be gentle, not to dismiss these comforting needs, and not only because Armchair too is richly supplied with pain fibres. I have my own stake in Armchair and Armchair's devotion. If Armchair stops being a fixture, I'll have to think long and hard about my own arrangements and my tender habit of spending as much time away from my lover as I possibly can. I do everything possible to look after him, short of being reliably there.

Whatever it is that ties us to each other, my lover and I, he is much too sensible to tug on it and see, once and for all, how much strain it will take. Much better to stay in doubt.

When I told my lover—he wasn't in hospital at the time—that I was thinking of spending half the week in Cambridge for a few months, he didn't say anything. It took him a while even to ask exactly how far away Cambridge is by train, and he seemed perfectly content when I said an hour and a bit—as if it counted as normal variation in a relationship, for one party to keep himself an hour and a bit away from the other. He didn't ask if I had some grand plan, like writing a textbook, which I think I mentioned once a while back as one of my ambitions. There's something very stubborn about his refusal to call my bluff.

He knows, of course, that part-timers don't have a lot of say in their timetables (part-timers least of all), so if I've managed to fit all my teaching this term into Monday, Tuesday and Wednesday, then I've been setting it up for months.

In Cambridge I stay in the flat of an actress friend who has a short-term contract with the RSC. She's staying with friends in London herself, and all she wants is for the place to be looked after. She warned me that she might come back for the odd weekend, but she hasn't shown up yet and I've stopped expecting her, stopped cleaning madly on a Friday and filling the fridge with fine things. So all I have to do is keep the place reasonably clean, water the plants and listen from time to time to her accounts on the phone of Barbican Depression and of understudy runs that the RSC potentates never stir themselves from the Seventh Floor to see. Her flat is very near the station, which keeps my guilt to a minimum. It's not as if I was holed up in Arbury or somewhere. I'm only an hour and a bit away.

What I do here, mainly, is take driving lessons. In anyone else, learning to drive—especially after thirty—would be a move so sensible no one would notice it. With me it's different. It's a sign of a secret disorder, a malady in its own right, but only I know that.

I've always set my face against learning to drive. I've used public transport as if I'd taken a pledge to do nothing else and have always been careful not to accept lifts unless I have to. You get superstitious about favours when you can't pay them back, not in kind. If someone who has offered me a lift stays on soft drinks, I find myself refusing alcohol as if that was a helpful contribution to the evening. It's probably just irritating. I dare say people think, if he likes his drink so little he'd make a handy chauffeur, why doesn't he get his bloody licence?

I seem to have based a fair bit of my character around not being a driver. Perhaps that's why I was so disoriented when I walked through the door of the driving school that first time. It felt like learning to swim, and this the deep end. But in all fairness, the air in there would give anyone's lungs pause. All the instructors smoke away at their desks when they're on phone-duty or doing paperwork, and there's a back room that's even smokier, with a sink and a dartboard and a little fridge, not to mention a tiny microwave and a miniature snooker table.

I must say I admire the way the driving school draws a new pupil smoothly into apprenticeship. I was given a time for a two-hour consultation with an instructor, who would suggest a test date. I was certainly impressed, and mainly with myself, the competent me they were hypothesizing so suavely. It'll take more than suavity to convince me that I'm viable as a driver, but I signed up for my session of consultation just the same, rabbit paralysed by the headlights, unable to disobey the order to climb into the driving seat.

Now that I'm familiar with the place, I can't help thinking that BSM stands for British School of Macho. There's only one woman in the place, who does paperwork the whole time and smiles at me with a forlorn sweetness. The rest of the staff, I imagine, conduct their job interviews in the pub, brusquely screening out non-drinkers, non-smokers, non-eaters of meat, non-players of pool, non-tellers of jokes. I imagine them rolling back with the candidate to the driving school after closing time for some cans of Special Brew, and I imagine them huddled outside the lavatory with their fingers to their lips, when he goes to relieve himself, listening for the clinching chuckle when he sees the HIGH FIRST TIME PASS RATE sign stuck up inside the lid. I imagine them giving each other the thumbs-up sign. And only then, after the candidate emerges from the lavatory, do I imagine them asking, 'By the way . . . can you drive?'

But somehow Keith, my instructor, slipped through their net. He does all the manly things, but he isn't a man in their sense, not at all. He's not a bachelor, but he's not by a long way a family man either, and he moved out of a perfectly nice house to live in a field.

He's a pleasantly runty fellow, brought up in a Barnardo's Home, and he still has a boyish spryness although he's in his late forties. To get from the driving school to the car, or back again at the end of the lesson, he bolts across Bridge Street, whatever the traffic's like, nipping through the smallest gaps between vehicles.

We set off in the driving school's sturdy Metro. It's white, but very dirty, so someone has been able to trace the words ALSO AVAILABLE IN WHITE in dust on the coachwork. The side mirrors are both cracked, and one is even crazed. I promise myself that I'll reward the car, if and when I finally pass, and not the examiner as is customary. I'll splash out on some replacement fixtures.

Towards Keith I have absurdly mixed feelings. I trust him blindly, and have for him the sort of disproportionately solid affection that goes with the analyst's couch more often than the steering-wheel. I admire his self-control. It's not that he doesn't get irritated—when I don't lose enough speed, for instance, approaching a roundabout—but he calms down right away. It's as if he was offering me an example, in terms of temperament, of the use of the gearbox, and how to lose momentum as efficiently as possible. When I stall, he says, 'Never mind, re-start,' without any hint that he's disappointed in me. As with any indulgent parental figure, I have an urge to test his patience to the limit, to make sure that he cares underneath it all.

Once the car ran out of petrol on Queens Road, but all I could think of when I lost power was that Keith had withdrawn his faith in me, and was overruling my accelerator with the brake on the passenger side. 'Are you braking?' I cried, and he said, 'No, I'm scratching my arse as a matter of fact,' before he realized I wasn't messing him about. We weren't far from the driving school, but he's so little of a walker that he insisted on staying put. We sat there, while his eyes flickered between the windscreen and his multiple mirrors, waiting for one of the other school cars to come by and give him a lift to the petrol station. No one came, and at last, with the light dying, we had to walk after all. But I was so pleased not to have made the mistake myself that I let slip a precious opportunity for mockery—which is pretty much Keith's natural language—and I didn't tease him at all. It was nice to be the one doing the forgiving.

Alongside the exaggerated trust I feel a sharp submerged resentment towards Keith and a desire to do something atrocious, like run someone over on a crossing, while he's taking responsibility for me. In reality, he would put the brake on in a second, but I imagine myself unfastening my seat-belt after the impact and walking away, never traced for some reason though the driving school has my details, and leaving Keith to deal with the consequences.

Sometimes he sets out to provoke me, as if he wanted to bring the crisis on. He murmurs, 'Closer, son, just a little closer, and you're mine,' when a child is playing too close to the road, and remarks on the economic advantage to parents of having a child wiped out sooner rather than later, before too much money has been spent on it. But I know this is just his style of cussedness, the same style that makes him answer 'no' in the back room of the driving school to the question, 'Got a light, Keith?' even when he's busy smoking away. It seems to be his solution, as a member of the artificial tribe of driving instructors, to the problem of how to be popular, without being despised for wanting to be liked.

Keith doesn't ask why I want to learn to drive. He takes it for granted, like everybody else, that I should, though in that case he should at least be curious about why it's taken me so long to get round to it. Even if he asked, I don't think I'd tell him my own theory on the subject: that it's to do with control, and also with risk. Anything that gives me the feeling of control is obviously going to come in handy at the moment, whether or not it's a sort of control that I have historically had any use for, but I think I'm also giving myself an education in risk. Being a pedestrian, being a passenger, isn't so very safe—and rattling around on a bicycle, as I do, isn't safe at all—but behind the wheel of a car you have a different relationship with the risks that you take.

I try not to keep secrets from my lover, but I don't talk a lot about what I do in Cambridge. I'm superstitious about that. I seem to think that if I talk to him more than vaguely about Cambridge, the seal will be broken and I'll start talking about him to the people I meet in Cambridge. For the whole cock-eyed arrangement to work, I need to think of the railway line from London to Cambridge as an elaborate valve, which allows me to pass from one place to another but strips me each time of my mental luggage and preoccupations.

The ward is full of its own life, and I don't think my silence shows. The patients tend to keep their doors open, so as to make the most of whatever passes along the corridors. The staff don't tell you when someone has died, but at least if your door is open someone comes along and says, with an apologetic smile, 'Let's just close this for a moment.' I expect that other people do what I do and peek out of the window in the door, which has horizontal bars of frosting so that I can't be seen, with any luck. I try to work out, from how long it takes for the trolley to make its collection, who it is that's inside it.

I'm sure I'm not the only one making calculations, though it's not a subject that comes up a great deal in conversation at the regular Tuesday tea parties. Then the focus of attention tends to be the chocolate cake brought in every week by an ex-patient, the offering that is richest in symbolism as well as in calories, which somehow always gets finished. Even my lover puts in his few bites' worth.

There's just one man on the ward who's in a different

category, a private patient who's recovering from a heart attack in a room that is costing his firm, or BUPA, £210 a day, not including the phone. He takes only short walks as yet, but sooner or later he'll come to the tea party or twig in some other way to what the problem is with everyone else in the ward. Once he asked my lover why he thought he had come down with this particularly nasty pneumonia. My lover just scratched his head, as if it had never occurred to him to wonder. But it's only a matter of time before the cardiac patient or his wife see two men holding hands. They'll be on that expensive telephone to BUPA right away, demanding to know why someone with a bad heart but otherwise good character has been sent to spend his convalescence in Sodom.

The day-room plays host to other events as well as the tea parties. There are the art classes and the Wednesday morning discussion groups. Often there's someone over by the window on these occasions, making faces and emitting harsh sighs, but if so it's just a patient strapped into the emetic aqualung of pentamidine grimacing with controlled disgust as he inhales through a mask filled with bitter gas. Sometimes it's even a discharged patient, coming back for a few lungfuls of fly-killer to keep the bugs at bay.

Through the open doors, at various times of the week, come the visitors who aren't quite friends. There's a manicurist, for one, who asks her clients, when she's finished, if they'd like a dab of nail polish. She quietens any protest by saying brightly, 'Some does and some doesn't, so I always ask.' The first time she offered her services to my lover, she'd broken her wrist and had her arm in a sling. She couldn't work, obviously, so what she was really offering was manicure counselling, rather than manicure as such. My lover said, to comfort her, 'I bite my nails anyway,' and she said, to comfort him, 'Well, you do it very well.'

An aromatherapist comes round from time to time to rub essential oils into people. She doesn't rub very hard, and my lover longs for a real massage, but it isn't easy telling her to be merciless. His pentamidine drip has brought his blood pressure right down, and it's easy to see how she might get the idea he should be handled with care—seeing he needs to be helped if he wants to go as far as the lavatory, which is three steps away. The aromatherapist takes away the pillows and blankets, and gets my lover to lie face down, with his feet where his head usually goes.

I get a shock every time I visit my lover after she has laid her too-gentle hands on him. It's as if there was some new symptom that could spin him bodily round, from end to end and top to bottom, and cast him down passive and aromatic, his eyes half-closed, on the crumpled sheets.

In the evenings, there are volunteers manning the hot-drinks trolley. They're noticeably more generous with the tea and the coffee than the domestics who push the trolley during the day, who can make visitors feel about as welcome as bedsores. With the evening trolley-pushers, I don't have to pretend that it's my lover who wants the drink if it's me who does really, and we don't scruple to ask for two if we're in the mood. The evening staff don't look right through me if I sit up on the bed next to my lover in my usual slightly infantile posture, facing the other way down the bed and hugging his big feet. This is the arrangement we've evolved now that so much of him is sore that a hug calls for as much careful docking as a refuelling in deep space. For him to see my face has become proportionally more important, as our bodies have had their expressiveness so much restricted.

My lover's soreness is dying down; I can tell because the fidgeting has gone out of his feet. I ask, in an interviewer's tenderly wheedling voice, 'What strikes you most about the whole terrible situation?'

Obligingly he answers, 'It brings out the best in people. And the worst.'

'What, you mean the best *and* the worst?'

'Both. The two.'

He's getting drowsy from the drugs he's on, as the chemical invasions of his body get the better of the surgical ones.

There's a hesitant knock on the door, and when I say to come in, this evening's volunteer stands in the doorway and asks what we want in the way of tea and coffee. I see him flinch when he spots the bag of blood on its wheeled stand, and the tube going into my lover's arm. But I notice too a quickening of interest in my lover, in the few seconds before our volunteer leaves the room to get the drinks from the trolley. Even before my lover murmurs, 'Isn't he gorgeous?' I have realized that the volunteer is very much my lover's type. He bears a passing resemblance to Joy Adamson's husband in the film of *Born Free*, a furry-faced scoutmaster on safari.

But now the volunteer returns with the teas and keeps his eyes turned down from the blood-drip. My lover has noticed his aversion and asks kindly, 'Does the blood bother you?'

'A bit.'

'Just a bit?'

'A lot.' Finally he admits that he sometimes feels faint. My lover looks affectionately at the sump of blood suspended above his arm and drawls, from the drastic languor of his medication, 'Just think of it as a big plastic kidney.' The volunteer resists the cue to look at the blood-bag, with the result that he continues to look deeply into my lover's eyes.

My lover pats the side of the bed. 'Do you have a moment to sit down?' I move over so that my lover can move his legs out of the volunteer's way, but my lover leaves his legs where they are, so the volunteer must make contact or else perch on the very edge of the bed.

The volunteer sits quiet for a moment, then clears his throat. 'Do you mind if I ask you a question?' he asks.

'Feel free,' my lover says. 'You're the guest.'

'Well, you're having a transfusion, and what I can never work out is, what happens to the blood you have extra, when you get someone else's on top of your own?'

'Yes, I used to wonder about that,' admits my lover. 'What happens is, they put another tube in your big toe, and drain the old blood out of there.' He gives the sheet a tug to loosen it from the bottom of the bed. 'Do you want a look?'

For the moment, the volunteer wants to go on looking at my lover's face.

'Don't you think you should?' my lover goes on. 'Shouldn't you try to overcome this silly fear of yours, if you're going to do the sort of work you're doing? Wouldn't that be the responsible thing?'

Mesmerized, the volunteer looks down at my lover's foot under the sheet. My lover pulls the sheet away from his foot. The big toe is pink and normal-looking. My lover looks startled and says, 'Oh, *Christ*, it must have come out, *now* we're in trouble, can you see it anywhere?' The volunteer casts his eyes desperately this way and that.

For some time I have been sending my lover signals of mild reproach about the wind-up job that is giving him so much pleasure; finally he gives in to them. He drapes the sheet over his feet again and says, 'Actually, since you ask, I pee away the surplus.' He smiles at the volunteer, who smiles back, at first incredulously and then with wonder at my lover's healthy sense of mischief.

My lover asks him please to tuck in the sheet round his feet, since it seems to have come adrift.

When the volunteer has gone at last, my lover says again, 'Isn't he gorgeous?' He looks thoughtful. 'But he can't be gay. That's never a gay beard. It's too overgrown.'

'I'm afraid you're right.'

'And you saw those corduroys.'

'Cords are a bad sign. Still . . . '

My lover sighs. 'At least he's not mutton dressed as lamb. He's mutton all right. But he has definite mutton appeal.' It sounds like an advert for stock cubes. 'He just can't be gay, that's all.'

My lover has a fantasy about living in the country with a vet who drives a half-timbered Morris Traveller, and this stranger comes close enough to set it off. A half-timbered Morris Traveller is apparently a car which even animals recognize as the appropriate vehicle for a person who will take care of them, so that they quieten down, even if their injuries are severe—or so my lover says—when they hear its engine note, some time before the car comes into view.

There is something I recognize as authentic in this fantasy of my lover's. It has about it the whiff of self-oppression, which we are as quick to recognize in each other as other couples, I imagine, are at spotting egg-stains on ties or lipstick on collars. The imaginary vet is classified by fantasy as virile and caring, in a way no man could be who loved other men, while my lover enters the picture as a damaged animal, a creature who can't hope to be treated as an equal but who accepts subordinate status as the price of tenderness.

All the same, the volunteer pays a number of return visits. He goes on holiday to Malta for a week and phones the hospital twice, so that the cordless phone—a treat that testifies to the volunteer's special status—is delivered to my lover's room, its aerial extended and gleaming. My lover has exercised once again his knack for being loved. The volunteer out of *Born Free*, meanwhile, is awarded a mark of privilege, a nickname: the Vet. Now my conversations with my lover have an extra layer of mysteriousness to nurses who hear me asking him if he's seen the Vet today. The Vet turns out to be older than he looks, in his mid-forties, so that he could almost be my lover's father. There's certainly something fatherly about the Vet when he sits on the bed and plays absent-mindedly with the hairs on my lover's leg. Sitting there, he might indeed be a father, trying to put off explaining the facts of life to an adolescent son, or a public-school housemaster explaining the meaning of confirmation.

One day I give my lover a bath; feeling clean, after all, is the nearest that people on this ward can come to feeling well. My lover is dizzy and unsteady on his feet, so I use a wheelchair to carry him back along the corridor to his room. I return the wheelchair to the bathroom right away, like a good boy, and the Vet must have arrived just while I was down the corridor, because when I come back I see that the door is closed. I look through the window and see the Vet perched on the bed, conducting his usual earnest conversation with my lover's leg. So I kill time doing a tour of the ward.

I offer to buy the patient in the room next to my lover's some of the ice-lollies he sucks when his mouth flares up, but he's well supplied at the moment, and his thrush doesn't even seem too bad. In fact he's unusually perky altogether. It was his birthday last week, and his ex-lover continued the custom they'd had by bringing him one practical present (a toasted-sandwich-maker) and one pampering present: a big bottle of essence of violets from Jermyn Street. I'm mean enough, by the way, to think that ex-lovers can afford to be generous; I look on them the way lifers in a prison must look on youngsters who are in for a short sharp shock.

The sandwich-maker was taken home, and the essence bottle was wrapped in a flannel and put by the basin, where a cleaner smashed it two days later. She burst into tears, and he told her not to worry about it, but in fact he wants to be reimbursed, and if the hospital doesn't have the relevant insurance he wants it taken out of the cleaner's wages. So now he's unpopular with the staff, but he's sticking to his guns. If dirty looks were radiotherapy he'd have lost a lot of hair by now, but the sense of defending a principle has given his health a definite boost.

When I return to my lover's room and peep through the window, the conversation shows no sign of stopping, so I leave them to it and go back to his neighbour's room, where the basin still smells like a florist's. There was something I glimpsed on the window sill a minute ago that puzzled me, and I summon up the nerve to ask about it.

It's a soft toy in the shape of a fat scheming cat, but a cat that seems to have two tiny hoops of wire fixed high on its stomach.

'That's my hospital Garfield,' explains the neighbour with a little embarrassment. 'I only use it in hospital.'

'No, I don't mean that,' I say, 'I mean, what are those?' I point at the little hoops.

He blushes outright and shyly opens his pyjama jacket. 'What you really mean is, what are these?'

His nipples have little inserted hoops of their own, and the hospital Garfield is indeed, as I thought incredulously at first glance, a soft toy with an erotic piercing.

My lover's neighbour nods at his customized toy. 'The nurses have this great sense of humour,' he says. 'They did that while I was out.'

I am slow to take in the information he is giving me. It is a few moments before I realize that by 'out' he means not just *socially unavailable* but *profoundly unconscious*.

I keep away from my lover as long as I plausibly can. Purely from a medical point of view, flirtation is likely to have a beneficial effect on his low blood pressure. A little teasing romance may actually make him stronger at the knees.

From my own point of view I feel not jealousy, but a definite tremor of worry. My lover's instinct for help is profound and I trust it. If he thinks I'm capable, then I am. But if he enlists the Vet, I lose confidence. It's not that I don't want to share the load. I'd love to. But if my lover is hedging his bets, then I suddenly fear that he has good reason. Perhaps he now realizes I will crack up or get ill myself. My equilibrium falters, and the glands of selfish worry, that I have been suppressing for the duration, flare up at once and all together.

On subsequent visits, the Vet consolidates his burly charisma in my lover's eyes by turning out to own the right cars. He doesn't drive a Morris Traveller as such—that would be a little bit spooky. But he does buy glamorous or gloriously dowdy cars cheap in auctions, and garages them with friends or in fields when they need a little more work than he can do, handy though he is. He drives an Alfa that costs him more in insurance every year than he paid in the first place. One of these days he knows that the police will pull him over and ask him ever so nicely not to wear it in public again. Waiting in various locations for a little more cash or an elusive spare part are a Bentley, an Aston Martin and a Wolseley.

My lover has a passion for fast and/or classic cars. Before I knew him he owned an MG—he put an old phone in it in fact, the kind you crank, and used to mime conversations at traffic-lights in summer, with the top down. This was before the days of car phones, let alone the days of commercially made imitation car phones—which I think makes it all right.

I don't follow my lover's car conversations with the Vet. I don't begin to understand what makes one car boxy but lovable, and another one nippy but a little Japanese about the hips.

There must be something about cars that makes people use a different register, almost a different language. Keith, my instructor, uses a whole mysterious vocabulary of phrases, so that I had to learn to understand his language, if not actually to speak Instructor, before I could really begin learning to drive. He mutters, 'Baby clutch . . . *baby* clutch,' when he wants me to be subtle with my left foot, and, 'Double gas . . . TREBLE gas,' when he wants me to be brash with my right. When I'm fumbling

141

between gears he prompts me ('then three . . . then two'), and when I've finally got it right and married speed to ratio, he says with mild put-on surprise, 'It works!' or else he gives a sort of jeer of approval ('Yeeeeah!'). If I don't need prompting for a minute or so, he'll murmur, 'Looking good' or, 'I'm almost impressed.' More often he gets me to slow down, with a warning 'Cool it,' or to speed up—for which he mutters, 'It's not happening' and makes gestures with his hands, sweeping them forwards.

I used to interpret the phrase and the gesture the wrong way, as if what Keith wanted was for the road to be taken away from in front of him, but I suppose that was just my old reluctance surfacing again in the lightest of disguises. I've got it worked out now and give the accelerator a squeeze. If I've been slow to understand him and deliver the speed he requires, Keith gets more direct. The phrases for this are 'Let's piss off out of here' or 'Give it a bit of poke.'

If I take my time before changing up, he goes 'mmmm', with a sharp intonation that says what-are-you-waiting-for? If I'm not properly positioned in my lane, he makes a flick of the hand to guide me in the right direction. Often, when I've misjudged a manoeuvre or underestimated a hazard, he says, with a quiet satisfaction, '*Not* a good gear.' To remind me of the mirror he sometimes taps it with his forefinger or mutters—there seems no obvious reason for his choice of language—'*Spiegel*'.

I start to relax in the lesson at the point where Keith lights up his first cigarette. I'm sure he's got enough of a craving that he'd light up sooner or later, whatever sort of idiot I was being, but I become more competent knowing he's felt able to focus his attention on the cigarette packet and the matches for a few seconds. Unless of course it's my terrible driving that makes the comfort of a cigarette so hugely attractive.

Keith opens the window a crack and leans forward to adjust the heating. I take every move he makes as a looming comment on my driving, so I'm absurdly relieved when he's only making adjustments to the car's interior climate. Then Keith talks. It's as if he's trying to simulate the distractions of traffic, when we're on a clear road. There's nothing I find harder than giving talking a low priority; left to my instincts, I'd rather be attentive in the conversation than safe on the road. It's not that I get flustered when he's really trying to put me off my stride—like the time he asked, 'When you going to get married, then?' after he had warned me he was about to request an emergency stop and before he actually smacked the dashboard to give me my cue. That question doesn't faze me, though I gather it's pretty much guaranteed to make the young men botch their manoeuvre. But I'm interested in Keith and what he has to say, and when he stops talking because there's tricky work ahead I can't wait to get the hazards behind me, whatever they are, and go back to what he's saying.

Sometimes Keith talks about nothing, anything, the daily papers, and how he's going to give up the *Sun* when they stop running their Bingo game—unless of course they announce another. He wrote a letter to the *Sun*'s Grouse of the Week column just recently, which they didn't print, complaining about a doctor in the news who'd overturned the car giving his daughter a driving lesson in the grounds of his house. It was taking a living away from driving instructors, that was Keith's Grouse, and served the doctor right, and what would *he* think if people started doing operations on each other in their kitchens?

Sometimes he talks about his history, about Barnardo's and the army and home-ownership.

'I had a lovely house in an acre, lovely car, two-car garage, garden with a rockery and floodlights—spent a grand on landscaping—fruit trees, currant bushes, but it wasn't what I wanted, none of it. I think I worked that out before I finished laying the rockery, but I still installed those bloody floodlights.'

He moved out from the house he shared with Sue and took up with Olga. Olga is the battered mobile home where he lives, parked in a muddy field a few miles out of town. She's a hulk, but he seems well set up there, in his way. We went out there once, on a lesson; I needed practice, apparently, manoeuvring in muddy conditions, and Keith certainly needed a Calor Gas container picked up and taken for refilling. We had a cup of tea in Olga while we were at it, though his eyes narrowed with distrust at the idea that anyone could drink it without sugar. He takes four spoonfuls and gives the tea-bag a good drubbing with the spoon, as if the point of the procedure was not to infuse a drink but actually to wash the tea-bag free of stains.

Laundry is one of the few services that he's not found a way of doing for himself. He does any telephoning he needs at the driving school, and even brings his electric razor in to work for re-charging with BSM current. He leaves the right change for milk and newspapers in Olga's mighty glove compartment and has them delivered right into her cab. But laundry is one thing that's beyond him and so he pops over to Sue's every week or so (and takes a bath while he's at it). He has 'a leg-over' while he's there, but to hear him talk about it, that leg-over isn't the lynch-pin of the arrangement. I imagine Sue in front of her mirror on one of the evenings Keith is expected—he doesn't always turn up, but he knows how to keep just enough on the right side of her that she doesn't come to find him, her horn sounding furiously all the way from the main road as her car crawls into the treacherous field where Olga sits. I imagine her powdering her face and wondering whether she should try some new perfume, not knowing it's Ariel that arouses Keith's senses, not Chanel.

I need a pee after my cup of tea. Keith shows me the lavatory, which is chemical and tucked away in a low cupboard. Keith can stand up in most parts of Olga, but there's nowhere that the roof's high enough to give my head clearance. To use the lavatory, I have to kneel and face forward. Keith gives me a little privacy by going to the cab, where he hasn't bothered to put up cork tiling. He presses a hand to the roof and says, 'Some mornings the condensation's unbelievable in here. It's like Niagara bastard Falls.'

Only when I'm finished with my rather awkward pee does he mention that personally, *personally*, speaking for himself, he finds it more convenient to piss in a bottle and then pour it away, though of course everybody's different, aren't they? There's a coffee jar, scrupulously clean and free of labels, tucked away at the side of the lavatory, which I suspect is his chosen bottle. I wish I'd spotted it earlier, though I doubt if I'd have had the nerve to use it.

Before we leave, Keith shows me his photo album. It's like anybody's photo album—anybody who wasn't thought worthy of a photograph before he joined the army, who built a raft in Malaya based on what people built in films when they were marooned, who had four children by two wives before there was ever a Sue, who kept sheep and chickens for a while in Devon—except that nothing's in order. It's the sort of album where each thick page has a thick sheet of Cellophane to hold the pictures down, no need of photo corners, and Keith seems to like keeping even the past provisional. Perhaps on non-bath evenings he amuses himself by rearranging the photographs, shuffling the blurred sheep and the precise soldiers, the blurred children. In every picture that shows Keith, he is pointing out of the frame, insisting that the real subject is out there somewhere, refusing to be the focus of the composition.

On the way back to town, he gets me to do some emergency stops. If it's at all possible, he synchronizes them with young women walking alone. He smacks the dashboard just before we pass. The woman usually glares at us as we stop dead right next to her and then she relaxes into a pitying half-smile when she sees it's only a learner driver, no real threat. Then her face goes half-way back to its original expression, when she sees that Keith is staring at her with a defiant hunger. At times like this, I am able to look at Keith outside the terms of our sealed-in little relationship, outside its flux of resentment and dependence, and he seems, I must admit, like a pretty ordinary little shit.

Even when I have passed my test and put Keith behind me, I can't imagine that I'll do a lot of driving. Public transport is enough to get me to the hospital, though I sometimes use my bicycle on a Sunday, partly for the exercise and partly to dramatize my errand, if I'm bringing something for my lover. On the bicycle I can feel like a courier whose package will make a difference to the person waiting for it.

My lover keeps the television on all the time, just turning up the sound when there's something he actually wants to watch. At the moment, a weatherman is standing in front of two maps of the country. I expect they represent the weather tonight and tomorrow. But the weatherman, if he wanted, could also show us the weather of our two healths. His vocabulary of symbols is meagre but it will stretch. My map will be full of smiling suns and light refreshing breezes, a fantasy of summer; my lover's map a nightmare winter, chock-a-block with gales and freezing showers. My lover looks without interest at the screen as it changes. Some of his calm is really exhaustion, but some of his calm is really calm. It helps that he's still in touch socially with the few people he exposed to risk. With a bravery that to me seems insane, they've all taken the test, and they all tested negative.

He keeps a list of his sexual partners, does my lover, though it's not so detailed he could use it to track people down if he'd lost touch. I only found out about it recently. It's at the back of his diary, but then I only found out about the diary recently. Suddenly there was this battered book on the bed, and my lover was saying, oh, yes, he always used to keep a diary, he'd just got out of the habit. He'd just now come across it and was taking a look.

Even my lover had to admit, after a little reading, that his diary-keeping had never been regular; he wrote in his diary only when a relationship was on the rocks. It took tears to get the words flowing and then he would write what were in effect letters to his lovers, full of sombre accusations and depressive spite. He even read me a detailed account of my own selfishness. This was his version of a crisis of which I have no version, since I survived it by not noticing.

I asked if I could look at the diary, and he passed it across. At the back of the book there was a list of numbers and names, starting with '1. John in Toyota Corolla.' Number two was Mark, and number three was Mark and Ben. The list went into the low forties before it met a scrawl, twice underlined: '*Enough of this rubbish.*' The list-making impulse had started to falter even before then. Two numbers in the thirties were entered as 'What was the name?' and 'Macho Letdown'.

My lover gave me a beady look as I read his diary and asked, 'Are you the sort of person who reads people's diaries?'

I didn't know there was any other sort of person, but I avoided the question by holding the book up and waving it. 'The evidence against me is strong.'

'I mean, when the owner's not around?'

'Only if I can find it.' I've only made a couple of searches since then—as much to see if he was bothered enough to hide it as because I'm curious—and I haven't found it, so I suppose the answer to the question is, Yes, he was bothered enough.

The limitations on my lover's future make his past the more precious, and I find that I'm a bit bothered, after all, that I don't know where his diary is.

I bring my lover hot thick soups, in a big old-fashioned vacuum flask with a wide neck. Conventional soups bear the same relationship to my soup as the sun bears to those collapsed stars whose every speck outweighs it. An oxtail is a wispy thing compared to what I make of it with the strong rendering of my pressure cooker. My soups are concentrated expressions of the will to nourish.

But tonight my lover is not to be nourished. 'You know I hate innards,' he says, pushing the plate of soup away almost as soon as I've poured it.

I'm ashamed that I don't know my lover's preferences as well as I should, but I'm also offended and I protest. 'Oxtail isn't innards!'

'It's as good as.'

'Oxtail couldn't be further from innards. Be reasonable. If cows kept their tails on the inside how would they deal with flies?'

Even as I say this, I realize that talk of flies is among the poorer triggers of appetite. The ward is full of tiny insects, as it happens, sustained out of season by the warmth and the abundance of fruit.

Even unmolested, the fruit would look incongruous beside the stack of moulded cardboard vomit-bowls on my lover's bedside table. They look, with their broad rims turned down at one side, like jaunty little hats, as if they were there for use in a big dance production number. We've tried to bring them into our private world by referring to them as 'Berkeleys' or 'Astaires', but the name that has stuck, *vomit-hats*, leaves them uncomfortably real. These homely objects resist the final push into euphemism.

Our little tussle over the soup reminds me of how poorly matched we are in habits and appetites. We don't even have the same taste in bread. I like wholemeal, but his stomach can deal most easily with inflated plastic white, and naturally I give way to him. All the same, I'd have thought somebody could make a killing out of couples like us, by producing a hybrid loaf that combined the two, all the goodness and bran sucked out of each alternate slice and shunted into the next one.

In this way among others, we don't present a united front. Our teamwork seems ragged, while the illness we're fighting is ruthlessly co-ordinated. But then it's only recently, since he came into hospital in fact, that I have thought of him, truly, as my lover.

Before then I compared him in my mind—often very flatteringly, it's true—with other men past or possible. But now I compare him only with the world as it will be when he is subtracted from it, not with rival beds but with his bed, empty. That is what locks the phrase in place: my lover.

M y lover and I never used pet names or endearments before his first visit to hospital, but how stupid it sounds when I say so. It's like saying *I never had much use for pot plants and cushions before I came to live in this condemned cell.* Except that the unstoppable progress of medical science has taken our condemned cell and turned it into a whole suite of condemned cells.

Our endearment system is based round the core-word *pie*, derived from the phrase *sweetie-pie* but given its independence in a whole series of verbal caresses. The turning-point in its history was my buying an Easter egg with the message piped on it, 'WITH LOVE TO MY SWEET PIE.' This was at a time when a raised patch on the roof of my lover's mouth had been diagnosed as a cancer, a separate sentence on his mouth that his tongue must read and remember every time it makes contact, and I wanted to go to meet him armed with more than a hug. It comforted me to watch the woman at Thorntons in Cambridge—where a free message in icing was a seasonal offer—at work on the egg with her expert nozzle of fondant and her smile of romantic voyeurism, a smile that would have hardened on her lips like painted sugar if she knew she was decorating a sweet to take the bitterness out of a malignancy.

Pie was the word that stuck, the last part of the inscribed egg that my lover would have eaten, I'm sure, if he hadn't kept the whole thing intact, as a totem of chocolate. *Pie* stuck to a number of phrases, private ones at first and then sentences of ordinary conversation, by slip of the tongue to start with and afterwards defiantly, mixing embarrassment and the refusal to be embarrassed. *Pie* functions as pet name (*dear one*), as interrogative (*are you awake?*), as exclamation (*how could you say such a thing!*).

So near have I approached to that which I vowed I would never use, the edged endearment of the grown-up, the *darling* of protest if not yet the *darling* of bitter reproach.

Pie is allied by assonance with *my* (*my Pie*), by alliteration with expressive adjectives: *poor Pie, precious Pie, pretty Pie*.

Occasionally it appears in phrases of estrangement, though its use acts as a guarantee that estrangement is reversible: *crusty Pie, poison Pie, piranha Pie*.

Written down and rationalized as an irrational number—π— it loses a little of its sugar. Transposed into fake Italian *mio Pio*—it acquires a register almost operatic. As a double diminutive—as *pielet* or *pilot*—it brings into play a fresh set of overtones.

Perhaps endearment, verbal sweetness so concentrated nothing else can survive, will prevent infection, the way honey does. Honey yanks the moisture out of bacteria with the violence of its osmosis. Honey has been found uncorrupt in the tombs of the Pharaohs, though it had been left there to be used, after all, to sweeten the darkness of the dead.

Who could have thought when the treasures were laid out in the vault that the bees' modest embalming would last so well, that their glandular syrup of flowers would turn out so nearly eternal?

My lover raises the remote control panel and turns the television off. Late at night, the nurses stop being so demanding, and even Armchair and the Vet can be relied on to stay away. My lover and I don't have to be so guarded in our behaviour.

This is the time we draft our imaginary letters to newspapers and public figures, our radical complaints and proposals. My lover wants to live long enough to be the only survivor of an air crash, so that he can say at the press conference, where he will have an arm in plaster, or perhaps only a finger, 'You see? God doesn't hate me after all, whatever *you* think.' In the meantime he will settle for composing imaginary letters to the papers, setting the record straight day by day.

Sometimes one or the other of us will shed some tears, but we haven't properly settled the agenda of our crying. We're both New Men, I suppose that's what it comes down to, so we have a lot of respect for tears and what they represent. Crying is a piece of expressive behaviour that needs no apology and isn't, absolutely isn't, a demand for attention. We pride ourselves on being able to ask for affection straight out, without needing to break down to do it. There's something a little crass about a hug as a response to tears. A hug can be an act of denial, even, and neither of us is going to make that mistake. We claim the right to cry uncomforted, letting the discharge do its work uninterrupted.

But in practice, I get so distressed by his tears, and he by mine, that we regress just as fast as we possibly can, and smother the expressiveness that we have so much respect for under a ton of hugs.

Endlessly we reformulate our feelings for each other. This is the same superstition that makes people put up bumper stickers—*Keep Your Distance*, *Baby on Board*, *I* ♥ *my* π—to make the roads safe and life go on for ever.

Fate is a dual-control Metro, that much I know, but I'm not clear about who's in which seat. It may be me, or it may be my lover, that squeezes the brake when we approach a bend too fast, or who pops the clutch in to prevent a stall. 'Baby clutch,' I can hear Keith saying in my ear, '*baby*-baby clutch,' as we move off up the hill to where we must go.

ROGER GARFITT
SUMMERS IN
NORFOLK

The front of the house was always in sunlight, the back in shadow. But the back had the water-butt, its soaked wood black and speckled with green mould. Rain-water was always used for the wash because it was softer and saved on soap powder, an economy of which I knew nothing. To me the water-butt was a presence. The shadow's core, it grew colder as you approached. A wet battery, a condenser, you could almost hear it hum.

The house had a cold tap in the scullery but no bathroom. Even this ordinary water was reserved, a kind of sacrament, to be heated in the kettle and carried up to the bedrooms. In the suburbs of London we were richer in convenience but poorer in ceremony. Entering the front bedroom we shared each summer with our parents was like entering a church. The door opened on to stillness and dark furniture. The water jug stood in a bowl on a white cloth on the wash-stand, the size of ritual vessels. The china was cold to the touch. It even smelled cold, like geraniums.

In the morning all was warmth and benediction. We would be brought tea and biscuits, and the jug would be taken down to be filled. It returned with a steam fragrance, a vapour that seemed lighter and thinner and sweeter than came from the hot tap at home. Washing had to be by turns, and we would hug the bed, dipping our biscuits in the tea until their half-soaked warmth merged with our half-sleep. When my mother called me up to the wash-stand, it was rather like taking communion, the same awkward intimacy, the same mixture of complicity and constraint. From my mother or my sister I would inherit warm, soapy water. An initial delicacy gave way to a sense of ease, as if I were still sharing my mother's blood-heat. It was rather like climbing into my sister's bath at home. But then came the constraint of not spilling any on the white cloth or the varnished top. The wash became, of necessity, ceremonial, a slow, deliberate laving.

Every so often we would be drummed into the ritual of Saturday night, which was bath night. A fire would be lit under the big copper, which had to be filled from the cold tap, bowl by bowl. The tin bath would be taken from its hook on the outside wall and laid on the rag rug in front of the kitchen range. Then the ladling would have to begin all over again, this time of hot water from the

153

copper. It was never quite the occasion it could have been. It was just expanding into privilege when I would be hurried along so that my sister could take over the water. More vividly than my own baths I remember the sense of being excluded from the comfort of the kitchen when my grandmother took hers. We would sit in the formality of the front room, conversing in hushed tones, as if awed by the extraordinary thought that Grandma was naked in the next room.

Food was cooked in the range but prepared in the long scullery that ran down to the back door and my grandmother spent much of her time there, out of sight. If I think back to the kitchen, it is to an absorbed silence, broken only by the turning of a page. I am curled in the crook of the couch, reading one of the copies of *Radio Fun* or *Film Fun* that still come for Billy and Peter, my grown uncles. Between my fingers I am twiddling a loose strand of the couch's black horsehair. My grandfather is in his armchair, deep in the *Eastern Daily Press*. Sometimes my parents' voices wash over our heads.

If my grandmother enters this memory, it is as a pair of hands. She has arthritis and, as she brings my grandfather a cup of tea, she does not hold the cup out, she holds it in, at a slight angle to her arm. The arm has the thinness of age, the skin falling away from the wrist and the knob of the wrist-bone and rucked into little folds around the elbow. But the skin is sandy and freckled, as if it has stored every hour of sun since April. Just as her hair, once the colour of barley wine, refuses to be white. Like corn bleaching in the sun, it prints lighter and lighter turns of gold, the only chemistry it knows. I watch her arms as she moves about the room, almost in love with their colour. As she reaches up for the biscuit tin on the mantelshelf, the muscles, still firm in their activity, draw into a ridge along the forearm, and the skin around the elbow tightens into a little whorl, almost decorative.

Sometimes, if she needed more room, if she was drawing a chicken or gutting rabbits, she worked on the end of the kitchen table. Then the fascination was to watch her fingers grope inside the chicken and draw out the string of unlaid eggs, diminishing from a shell-less egg complete in its skin to a tiny bead of yolk, an orange match-head burning inside a blood-red membrane. She used the shell-less egg for the stuffing and almost everything else except the intestines, which were rapidly bundled into newspaper and incinerated in the range. She pulled out the gizzard, slit its little bag and cleaned away the grit the chicken used as an internal mill to grind up its corn. At this point we always tensed ourselves, expecting the grey sludge to smell like the intestines, but the little stones were clean and fresh, like rain-washed gravel. She cut the feet off, scalded them in boiling water, and scraped off the claws and scales, starting at the toes and whittling down the leg. Then boiled gizzard and feet together to make gravy. As she detached the foot and pulled the sinews out of the thigh, the chicken clenched its toes. This appalled us, and we were given the foot to see how it worked. We pulled at the dangle of sinews until we found the string that operated the toes. We had a horror from the Ghost Train, three cold claws that could pluck at your sleeve, or tickle an adult's neck as they read the newspaper. It became a regular game, a ghostly cock-fight in which two disembodied feet leaped and spurred at each other until it was time to give up their jelly to the gravy.

More often, though, my grandmother was off in the scullery, and in the kitchen we sat in my grandfather's warm. This is just how it felt. It warmed you simply to look at my grandfather. He was like a coal in a well-laid fire, burning in its own heat, a white, steady glow. Perhaps I saw him at the age to which he was best suited. Already, in the earliest photo I have of him, a man still short of fifty, holding me up to the camera as a babe in arms, he was well set in the mould: white toothbrush moustache, flat cap and raincoat. Summer might change the flat cap to a straw hat and the raincoat to a light grey jacket: but nothing disturbed the considered movements or ruffled the voice. Perhaps it was his voice that reassured us. Norfolk voices are quick and slightly singsong, swooping up interrogatively at the end of the sentence. He was a Yorkshireman, and still left himself time for broad vowels, though he had lost their breadth over the years. His voice moved like a river in a backwater, in a slow brown swirl. He grumbled and chuckled but my Aunt Ruth only once heard him laugh outright. She was keeping watch by his last bed, as he was dying of cancer. In his delirium he was back marching with the British Legion. Suddenly he laughed and said, 'Yes, we've been married six weeks.'

We always felt immensely comfortable in his presence. Perhaps because he was companionable, talking to us over a late breakfast before he puttered off on his Autocycle to Sedgeford, where he had a shoe-repairer's shop on the Heacham Road, a little lean-to shed beside a petrol pump which he minded for the garage down the bank. He had a weak stomach and great care was taken over his food. His Shredded Wheat came with warm milk. We preferred ours cold: warm milk smelled of cow's breath and udders. On cold days we had porridge, made in the Scots fashion with salt, and with the milk added afterwards, floating in a thin rim round the plate. Grandad always stirred a spoonful of Fowler's Black Treacle into his, and recommended us to do the same. Good for the health, he said. We stared in disbelief as the porridge turned brown and took on a bitter taste, far too strong for us.

Rushworth he was called, Rush for short, which made the family smile. A stubborn little badger of a man, there was no hurrying him and he was easily delayed. He took so long to persuade into a day's outing that the day was lost. Painstaking at his craft, he took pains to the point where they impoverished him, putting more time into a boot's reparation than he could possibly charge for. He rarely refused anyone credit, even if they still owed from last time. And yet to see him at his overcrowded work-bench behind small dim panes of glass was to see a man who had found his freedom, a man patching and piecing and perfecting in his own time.

Later, when we had moved to a farm and he stayed with us there, he spent his visit in the shed, sorting through the extraordinary tangle of tools on the bench. The old farmer had been a considerable craftsman, as well as a collector of odds and ends: a Colt 45 revolver, an ancient .22 pistol used for shooting rats, a German commando knife still wickedly sharp and nestling in the grease of its sheath. At the end of the fortnight Grandad emerged to announce that he had sorted all the loose screws and nails into sized and labelled boxes. 'I'll sort the rest out next year,' he said.

Only now, looking back, can I see that his indulgence of us, the warmth that seemed to flow from him, flowed in part from my grandmother's indulgence of him. Both of them had worked hard to raise five children through the Depression. For twenty years he did a postal round as well as his boot and shoe repairs and attended to hardship cases for the Legion on Sundays. But the income from his small trade would never have been enough if my grandmother had not turned their front room into a fish and chip shop in winter and an ice-cream parlour in summer. Between times she dug the vegetable garden, raised rabbits and hawked fresh fish around the countryside on her bike. Once she even tried to use his motorbike: he showed her how to start it but forgot to show her how to stop and she crashed into the neighbour's gate two doors down.

A cinder path ran along the backs of the terrace, taking on a different shading from each household as it went. Then it turned into the road itself, which was like a dried riverbed of sand and gravel, pot-holed and patched. This, we were told, was an unadopted road. To us its wayward, wandering surface was an immense liberation. Each year the holiday seemed to begin as the car tyres turned off the council's Tarmac and scrunched across it. The engine note changed, the wheels surged across sandbanks and wallowed down into dips, as if we were already driving along the track to the beach. Woodend Road it was called, a cul-de-sac that petered out into a vagueness of trees. We seemed to have turned off the map.

All sorts of oddities persisted along Woodend Road, informal arrangements that would certainly have been breaches of the planning regulations, had they applied here. One bungalow had a builder's yard beside it, where a small contractor kept his stacks of bricks. Opposite us lived the Floods, who parked their removals van in a field behind the house. Lying awake on light summer nights, we would hear the sound of the van returning and peep through the curtains. It would be right below us, its blunt whale snout up against our gate and its dark hump stranded across the road. We could see Mr Flood in the cab, white-haired and slightly flushed in the face. He would lean out of his seat, peering down at the fence on either side, while younger Floods—brothers, sons, nephews—tumbled out of the lorry and took up watchful positions fore and aft. There was a familiar tension to this manoeuvre, a near-impossibility that filled them with a kind of elation. Banter flew back and forth, mostly at the expense of Mr Flood. His head jerked back and his grin broadened with each new sally. It was his daily acclamation as patriarch. I never saw anyone else at the wheel.

He took his bearings and then went into a frenzy of tight turns and reversings, hauling on the wheel, stamping on the clutch, tugging at the gear-lever. He flung himself into it as if he could swing the lorry around before the laws of the universe caught up with him. Just before the bumper touched, an amused *Whoa!* would come from one of his assistants. Once the shout came a fraction late and the bumper toppled our gatepost. Mr Flood descended from the cab with a slow smile and with his status, if anything, enhanced. Toppling gateposts was his prerogative.

Our eccentricity was that the front garden held the neat, brown, upright shape of the Maggot, Grandad's Austin Seven. He had hinged the front fence so that it folded back, enabling him to drive the Maggot on to the little square of gravel. Once the fence was drawn across again, the Maggot looked like a Matchbox model in its matchbox. It shone along its short brown bonnet and gleamed around its black mudguards. The radiator cap was just like the cap on the waste-pipe below the sink, a plain round of metal with two uprights for spanner grips, but the Maggot wore it as proudly as a Bentley wears its winged B. Clearly it had never heard its own nickname, which may have come from the way the black hood concertina'd and stretched into a series of little ridges, like a maggot humping itself along, or may simply have referred to the car's comically small proportions. The Maggot was like a Jack Russell or a bantam cock, undiminished in its own eyes.

But then it stood in a charmed circle. It was the first car my grandfather had ever owned and the first car I remember riding in as a child. It becomes hard to distinguish my sense of novelty from my grandfather's. Or to separate the affection I felt for the Maggot from the affection I felt for him. But I sense that the circle's hub, its binding spell, may be the respect with which my grandfather treated all tools and machinery, from the old foot-treadled machine with which he stitched uppers, to the electric finishing machine that burred around newly fastened soles and heels. Nothing was ever thrown away: a long boot-knife that had worn thin and snapped would be sharpened up again into one of the little pointed knives he always had ready to hand. The latest machines were bought as soon as they came out, and his Junker sole-sewer held pride of place: but he still took the time to temper soles by running them through his old set of rollers, just as when he sewed them by hand. Rarely with him in his workshop, I was often with him in the Maggot, spellbound by the stateliness he gave that little vehicle. Perhaps there I came closest to glimpsing the world through his eyes—if glimpse is the word for an unhurried vision in which the simplest objects, flawed as they might be, seemed to possess their own dignity.

The Maggot sat bolt upright on its chassis, rather as Great Granny Edwards, the one time I saw her, sat stiffly on her chair, all the more rigid for being a little shaky. As soon as Grandad opened the passenger door, we knew we were entering a presence. There was an emanation of warm, polished leather, a smell of decorum. Small children, clambering into the back over a tipped-down seat, we composed ourselves. Even when Grandad pressed that starter, a round plug set in the floor, and it gave an accelerating gurgle like water going down the plug-hole, composure was not broken. Not even when the plug ran dry and Grandad had to crank the little car so that it trembled under our feet. Gravely he descended from the driving seat and bent to the starting handle. His movements, always slow, became almost priestly in their reassurance. Give it time, he seemed to be saying, give it time.

He treated the engine rather as he treated his own delicate stomach: it was not to be unsettled. He let it steady to its beat before engaging first gear. Then moved off slowly, allowing it to rebuild its rhythm. It did not rattle, it shook. We could hear the small, controlled explosions, the successive rips of compression, going off like lines of caps. We watched Grandad listening, judging the moment to change up again. This was a matter of profound deliberation. Each gear had a chapter to itself; every corner was like rounding Cape Horn. He steered rather as a bus driver steers a double-decker, passing the wheel from hand to hand, and the radiator cap on the little bonnet swung like a compass needle across the window panes of the Co-op or butted around the curve of the wall opposite the Wheatsheaf.

What I remember of journeys with my grandfather is that they lasted longer than other journeys. A quarter of a mile to the shops stretched in time and became an epic of small events. The High Street floated by, as clear in each detail as if it was under a magnifying glass. The effect of this, paradoxically, was to magnify the Maggot itself. I looked out over the curve of the driver's seat, past the back of my grandfather's neck, thick white hairs under the rim of a brown tweed cap, to the window frame and the sharp edges beyond, gateposts and walls and house-ends, suddenly aware of this small lounge in which we were travelling through space, the leather sofa and varnished woodwork my grandfather had to steer between buildings and bring safely to rest at the kerb.

Rushworth Garfitt, 1895–1966
Florence Edwards, 1889–1968

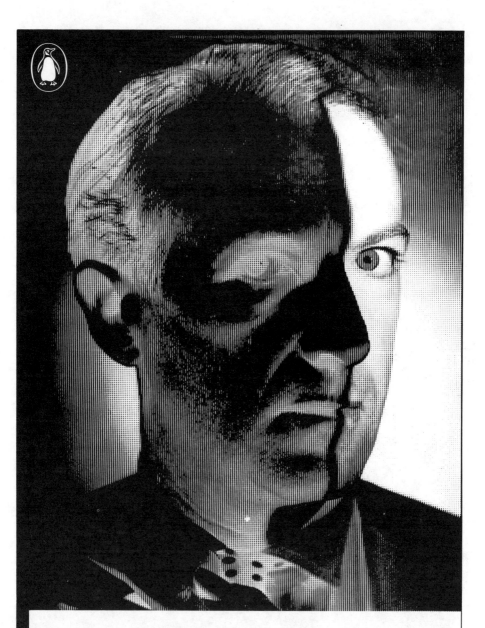

PENGUIN TWENTIETH-CENTURY CLASSICS

Cecil Beaton by Erwin Blumenfeld,
reproduced by courtesy of the San Francisco Museum of Modern Art and Kathleen Blumenfeld.

MICHAEL IGNATIEFF
DEFICITS

It begins the minute Dad leaves the house.

'Where is George?'

'He is out now, but he'll be back soon.'

'That's wonderful,' she says.

About three minutes later she'll look puzzled: 'But George . . .'

'He's away at work, but he'll be back later.'

'I see.'

'And what are you doing here? I mean it's nice, but . . .'

'We'll do things together.'

'I see.'

Sometimes I try to count the number of times she asks me these questions but I lose track.

I remember how it began, five or six years ago. She was sixty-six then. She would leave a pot to boil dry on the stove. I would discover it and find her tearing through the house, muttering, 'My glasses, my glasses, where the hell are my glasses?'

I took her to buy a chain so that she could wear her glasses around her neck. She hated it because her mother used to wear *her* glasses on a chain. As we drove home, she shook her fist at the windscreen.

'I swore I'd never wear one of these damned things.'

I date the beginning to the purchase of the chain, to the silence that descended over her as I drove her home from the store.

The deficits, as the neurologists call them, are localized. She can tell you what it felt like when the Model T Ford ran over her at the school gates when she was a girl of seven. She can tell you what a good-looking man her grandfather was. She can tell you that her grandmother used to say, 'A genteel sufficiency will suffice,' when turning down another helping at dinner. She remembers the Canadian summer nights when her father used to wrap her in a blanket and take her out to the lake's edge to see the stars.

But she can't dice an onion. She can't set the table. She can't play cards. Her grandson is five, and when they play pairs with his animal cards, he knows where the second penguin will be. She just turns up cards at random.

He hits her because she can't remember anything, because she keeps telling him not to run around quite so much.

Then I punish him. I tell him he has to understand.

He goes down on the floor, kisses her feet and promises not to hit her again.

She smiles at him, as if for the first time, and says, 'Oh, your kiss is so full of sugar.'

After a week with him, she looks puzzled and says, 'He's a nice little boy. Where does he sleep? I mean, who does he belong to?'

'He's your grandson.'

'I see.' She looks away and puts her hand to her face.

My brother usually stays with her when Dad is out of town. Once or twice a year, it's my turn. I put her to bed at night. I hand her the pills—small green ones that are supposed to control her moods—and she swallows them. I help her out of her bra and slip, roll down her tights and lift the nightie over her head. I get into the bed next to hers. Before she sleeps, she picks up a Len Deighton and reads a few paragraphs, always the same paragraphs, at the place where she has folded down the page. When she falls asleep, I pick the book off her chest and I pull her down in the bed so that her head isn't leaning against the wall. Otherwise she wakes up with a crick in her neck.

Often when I wake in the night, I see her lying next to me, staring into the dark. She stares and then she wanders. I used to try to stop her, but now I let her go. She is trying to hold on to what is left. There is a method in this. She goes to the bathroom every time she wakes, no matter if it is five times a night. Up and down the stairs silently, in her bare feet, trying not to wake me. She turns the lights on and off, smooths a child's sock and puts it on the bed. Sometimes she gets dressed, after a fashion, and sits on the downstairs couch in the dark, clutching her handbag.

When we have guests to dinner, she sits beside me at the table, holding my hand, bent forward slightly to catch everything that is said. Her face lights up when people smile, when there is laughter. She doesn't say much any more; she is worried she will forget a name and we won't be able to help her in time. She doesn't want anything to show. The guests always say how well she does. Sometimes they say, 'You'd never know, really.' When I put her to bed afterwards I can see the effort has left her so tired she barely knows her own name.

She could make it easier on herself. She could give up asking questions.

'Where we are now, is this our house?'

'Yes.'

'Where is our house?'

'In France.'

I tell her: 'Hold my hand, I'm here. I'm your son.'

'I know.'

But she keeps asking where she is. The questions are her way of trying to orient herself, of refusing and resisting the future that is being prepared for her.

She always loved to swim. When she dived into the water, she never made a splash. I remember her lifting herself out of the pool, as sleek as a seal in a black swim-suit, the water pearling off her back. Now she says the water is too cold and taking off her clothes too much of a bother. She paces up and down the poolside, watching her grandson swim, stroking his towel with her hand, endlessly smoothing out the wrinkles.

I bathe her when she wakes. Her body is white, soft and withered. I remember how, in the changing-huts, she would bend over as she slipped out of her bathing-suit. Her body was young. Now I see her skeleton through her skin. When I wash her hair, I feel her skull. I help her from the bath, dry her legs, swathe her in towels, sit her on the edge of the bath and cut her nails: they are horny and yellow. Her feet are gnarled. She has walked a long way.

When I was as old as my son is now, I used to sit beside her at the bedroom mirror watching her apply hot depilatory wax to her legs and upper lip. She would pull her skirt up to her knees, stretch her legs out on the dresser and sip beer from the bottle, while waiting for the wax to dry. 'Have a sip,' she would say. It tasted bitter. She used to laugh at the faces I made. When the wax had set, she would begin to peel it off, and curse and wince, and let me collect the strips, with fine black hairs embedded in them. When it was over, her legs were smooth, silky to touch.

167

Now I shave her. I soap her face and legs with my shaving brush. She sits perfectly still; as my razor comes around her chin we are as close as when I was a boy.

She never complains. When we walk up the hill behind the house, I feel her going slower and slower, but she does not stop until I do. If you ask her whether she is sad, she shakes her head. But she did say once, 'It's strange. It was supposed to be more fun than this.'

I try to imagine what the world is like for her. Memory is what reconciles us to the future. Because she has no past, her future rushes towards her, a bat's wing brushing against her face in the dark.

'I told you. George returns on Monday.'

'Could you write that down?'

So I do. I write it down in large letters, and she folds it in her white cardigan pocket and pats it and says she feels much less worried.

In half an hour, she has the paper in her hand and is showing it to me.

'What do I do about this?'

'Nothing. It just tells you what is going to happen.'

'But I didn't know anything of this.'

'Now you do,' I say and I take the paper away and tear it up.

It makes no sense to get angry at her, but I do.

She is afraid Dad will not come back. She is afraid she has been abandoned. She is afraid she will get lost and never be able to find her way home. Beneath the fears that have come with the forgetting, there lie anxieties for which she no longer has any names.

She paces the floor, waiting for lunch. When it is set before her, she downs it before anyone else, and then gets up to clear the plates.

'What's the hurry?' I ask her.

She is puzzled. 'I don't know,' she says. She is in a hurry, and she does not know why. She drinks whatever I put before her. The wine goes quickly.

'You'll enjoy it more if you sip it gently.'

'What a good idea,' she says and then empties the glass with a gulp.

I wish I knew the history of this anxiety. But I don't. All she will tell me is about being sprawled in the middle of Regent Street amid the blood and shop glass during an air raid, watching a mother sheltering a child, and thinking: I am alone.

In the middle of all of us, she remained alone. We didn't see it. She was the youngest girl in her family, the straggler in the pack, born cross-eyed till they straightened her eyes out with an operation. Her father was a teacher and she was dyslexic, the one left behind.

In her wedding photo, she is wearing her white dress and holding her bouquet. They are side by side. Dad looks excited. Her eyes are wide open with alarm. Fear gleams from its hiding place. It was her secret and she kept it well hidden. When I was a child, I thought she was faultless, amusing, regal. My mother.

She thinks of it as a happy family, and it was. I remember them sitting on the couch together, singing along to Fats Waller records. She still remembers the crazy lyrics they used to sing:

> *There's no disputin'*
> *That's Rasputin*
> *The high-falutin loving man.*

I don't know how she became so dependent on him, how she lost so many of the wishes she once had for herself and how all her wishes came to be wishes for him.

She is afraid of his moods, his silences, his departures and his returns. He has become the weather of her life. But he never lets her down. He is the one who sits with her in the upstairs room, watching television, night after night, holding her hand.

People say: it's worse for you, she doesn't know what is happening. She used to say the same thing herself. Five years ago, when she began to forget little things, she knew what was in store, and she said to me once, 'Don't worry. I'll make a cheerful old nut. It's you who'll have the hard time.' But that is not true. She feels everything. She has had time to count up every loss. Every night, when she lies awake, she stares at desolation.

What is a person? That is what she makes you wonder. What kind of a person are you if you only have your habits left? She can't remember her grandson's name, but she does remember to shake out her tights at night and she never lets a dish pass her by without trying to clean it, wipe it, clear it up or put it away. The house is littered with dishes she is putting away in every conceivable cupboard. What kind of a person is this?

It runs in the family. Her mother had it. I remember going to see her in the house with old carpets and dark furniture on Prince Arthur Avenue. The windows were covered with the tendrils of plants growing in enormous Atlas battery jars, and the parquet floors shone with wax. She took down the giraffe, the water buffalo and the leopard—carved in wood—that her father had brought back from Africa in the 1880s. She sat in a chair by the fire and silently watched me play with them. Then—and it seems only a week later—I came to have Sunday lunch with her and she was old and diminished and vacant, and when she looked at me she had no idea who I was.

I am afraid of getting it myself. I do ridiculous things: I stand on my head every morning so that the blood will irrigate my brain; I compose suicide notes, always some variant of Captain Oates's: 'I may be gone for some time.' I never stop thinking about what it would be like for this thing to steal over me.

She has taught me something. There are moments when her pacing ceases, when her hunted look is conjured away by the stillness of dusk, when she sits in the garden, watching the sunlight stream through all the trees they planted together over twenty-five years in this place, and I see something pass over her face which might be serenity.

And then she gets up and comes towards me looking for a glass to wash, a napkin to pick up, a child's toy to rearrange.

I know how the story has to end. One day I return home to see her and she puts out her hand and says: 'How nice to meet you.' She's always charming to strangers.

People say I'm already beginning to say my farewells. No, she is still here. I am not ready yet. Nor is she. She paces the floor, she still searches for what has been lost and can never be found again.

She wakes in the night and lies in the dark by my side. Her face, in profile, against the pillow has become like her mother's, the eye sockets deep in shadow, the cheeks furrowed and drawn, the gaze ancient and disabused. Everything she once knew is still inside her, trapped in the ruined circuits—how I was when I was little, how she was when I was a baby. But it is too late to ask her now. She turns and notices I am awake too. We lie side by side. The darkness is still. I want to say her name. She turns away from me and stares into the night. Her nightie is buttoned at the neck like a little girl's.

GRANTA 10: TRAVEL WRITING

Redmond O'Hanlon
INTO THE HEART OF BORNEO

Paul Theroux
SUBTERRANEAN GOTHIC

Martha Gellhorn
WHITE INTO BLACK

Patrick Marnham
HOLY WEEK

Bruce Chatwin
A COUP

Jonathan Raban
SEA-ROOM

Jan Morris
INTERSTATE 281

Also in this issue: Gabriel García Márquez, Russell Hoban, Norman Lewis, Colin Thubron, Saul Bellow, Todd McEwen and others.

'It's the finest prose anthology for years.'
New Statesman

Granta 10 is again available at £5.00 from Granta, FREEPOST, Cambridge CB1 1BR.

JOHN TREHERNE
HEART

They put me in a wheelchair and draped a shawl around my shoulders, a woollen, cellular one—the kind they use in babies' prams. The chair wheels wouldn't turn properly at corners, and it was unbearably hospital hot. There were posters about AIDS and shrivelled-looking men with pipes coming out of their heads.

I had only called in for a check-up on the way to work.

After X-rays, they shoved me into bed and stuck a three-way tap in my arm. A green television screen blipped over my head. Electrode jelly stuck to the hairs on my chest. If you jiggled the wires, the television blips jumped up and down.

'Coffee or Horlicks, dear?' A middle-aged woman in a fawn check dress regarded me in a detached way, spoon poised.

A nurse appeared. 'Uncross your ankles,' she ordered. 'It's bad for your peripheral circulation.' She had neat ankles, I noticed, and large, luminous eyes; in her early thirties she might have been and looked as though she was married. I was feeling ridiculous. I was in intensive care, she said, in the Cardiac Unit.

The man in the next bed was also wired up. His television blips looked terrible. He had come in the night before, he said. He was a widower, came from New Zealand a long time ago, and was worried about his Yorkshire terrier, which was locked in the bungalow, *and* about his cheque-book, which he had left on a window-sill. And he was feeling hot. He looked hot: it was hot—*I* was hot. But he was getting hotter and looking decidedly queer.

They pulled curtains around him. The pretty nurse ran in carrying a metal suitcase. It was too heavy for her; she held her tummy afterwards. There were more running feet, then gurglings and a regular metallic thumping behind the curtains.

I tried to read Bruce Chatwin's *Utz*. The terrible noises stopped.

When they drew the curtains, the bed was empty.

The next arrival was much younger: forty-eight, he told the nurse when she filled out his form, and had two children. He smoked thirty a day, he said, and evidently drank a good deal. The pains had started a few days before and had got worse after

Photo: Henri Cartier-Bresson (Magnum)

breakfast. He was feeling hot too. They drew his curtains. There
were those noises again—then silence.

Sister sent a nurse in case I was upset. She sat and put an
arm round me at the very moment a familiar college figure
appeared at the end of the bed. It was the Master. He gave me a
funny look—and a copy of the *Economist*. We chatted about
goings-on at the High Table.

My visitors looked uncomfortable when I tried to tell them
about my ward-mates and the manner of their passing. I should
not dwell on such things, they said. It was morbid and would do
no good. Of course someone would look after the Yorkshire
terrier. They would find a television set for me. And would bring
more books.

But I was now much possessed by death and saw beneath the
skin.

The next day they wheeled me out of Death Row, along with
my rapidly accumulating belongings. Everyone declared that they
had never seen so many flowers, so many get-well cards, such
piles of fruit. And all those books!

They talk to you like that when you come out of intensive
care.

I was struggling with Peter Carey's *Oscar and Lucinda*—I
must have had the entire Booker short-list—when that nice
consultant and his attendants reappeared. He had pored over
charts of my heartbeats and said that I was looking much better.
But I'd had a heart attack right enough. What is more, they knew
when. Seven days before I went into intensive care it must have
been, they reckoned. Couldn't I recall feeling queer? About
seven days before I came in?

Now that they mentioned it, that day had been a real daisy:
more Thatcher cuts for my research group; the meeting with the
architect in my now near-derelict home to discover more dry rot.
Then a visit to the undertakers to collect my old friend's ashes for
scattering. I had plodded through the college swinging the plastic
shopping-bag, and it was when I was eating lunch that I noticed
the ash on my sleeve—I *suppose* like a rose might also leave—
and felt terrible. No pains, just terrible.

The houseman came back later and drew pictures to show where cuts could be made, tubes inserted. My world began to wobble. I was back on Death Row.

But I was out again the next day.

The nurse who came with me in the ambulance was Texan. She said that her aunt had fixed Bonnie Parker's hair when she blew into Wichita Falls with Clyde Barrow. That would have been in the summer of 1932, I calculated as the sunlit A45 verge and hovering motorway kestrels slipped by. Did she mean her great-aunt, I wondered? Perhaps she was older than she looked. Was my memory going? Ah, well! At least Bonnie had a quick end at Gibsland, Louisiana. No languishing in a hospital bed with wires stuck to her. Where did you stick them on a woman's chest, anyway?

The new nurses were impressive. Tall, golden young women, with kind eyes and soft voices. No larking about, just gentle talk of this and that in my own sunny little room, with views of ducks and falling leaves, as they patiently recorded my temperature and blood pressure.

I began to develop an equivocal attitude towards the pulsating object on which my life depended. Its loyalty was suspect. Worse, it now seemed rather sinister. Like a captive organism—a decerebrate squid or some other fleshy invertebrate—it pounded away in the middle of my chest, following its own mindless fate to which mine was inextricably linked.

The question I pondered, though, was what 'they'—or, more precisely, the consultant—had in mind to do. Transplant? Bypass? Bloody great scars down the middle of your chest? I'd seen some of *those* when I had been taken off for some of my tests.

My visitors, who were now quite numerous, began to wonder as well. When do you think they will do anything? Any news of the treatment? A chap in Peterhouse had a bypass. Fit as a fiddle he was afterwards. *Surely* they will be telling you something soon.

The consultant appeared twice, with white-coated satellites. He had an absorbed way of looking at me—like a dipterist examining an interesting pinned specimen—except when he became conscious that I was staring at him: then he relaxed. He was kind and smiled frequently. He favoured 'non-invasive' treatment, he said. And so did I. It was just a matter of swallowing pills until they hit the right combination. And when they did I said goodbye and was driven across a cold, green landscape into winter when I thought it was still autumn.

WILLIAM COOPER
A HISTORY

'I don't want to leave you all.' She paused. 'It seems so soon . . .' She was my wife, and I was sitting beside her bed in a ward of the Westminster Hospital. The ward had a name, after some illustrious benefactor; it was in effect the cancer ward. To begin with, she had been treated there over the last two years as an out-patient; she had now been an in-patient for ten weeks. What she was saying was recognizing that she was never going to come out, that she was going to die. She was going to leave us all.

'It seems so soon . . .' She was fifteen years younger than me—when I married her I was forty, she only twenty-five. Since then we had lived through thirty-eight years of close and happy marriage. After a succession of false-starts preceding it, I could only take it as an enduring stroke of luck, inexplicable in terms of reason. (She always said I was the most interesting man she had ever met; in return I said she always knew how to make a man of me.) There it was, a lasting refuge and joy to us. I had married her as a pretty girl: ageing had transformed her into a beautiful woman . . . We had of course lived conscious of the fifteen years' difference in our ages, had sometimes discussed how she was to cope with a protracted widowhood. Now it was she who was going to go first, with me aged seventy-seven and her only sixty-two. 'It seems so soon . . .' It was.

'You all' meant me and our two daughters. We loved each other dearly and between ourselves easily demonstrated our affection. Both daughters were unmarried, the elder living at home with us, the younger living with a young man on the far side of London yet often telephoning and coming to see us. We all found it easy to embrace each other whenever or wherever we met; and it came naturally to me to tell my wife frequently that I loved her, and she told me that she loved me—which was the truth. I had lived steadily in the glow of it, until just recently when I happened to read in an authoritative newspaper article—the writer himself was suffering from cancer—that 'the typical cancer sufferer' is one who is frustrated, suppressing anger. Whether or not there is some element of genetic inheritance in the disease—my wife's father died of it—I have since failed to keep the idea out of my thoughts . . . Was my wife in some way frustrated, repressing anger? If she was, the cause must be me. Anger against the limitations, a distantness and absence of 'give' in my temperament? Frustrated by a strand of the overbearing in me—as for example in my insisting on her giving up a career when we married? It's now too late to know, still less to explain; I doubt if words go deep enough, anyway. She died on the thirtieth of May 1988, over a year ago. I think of her innumerable times a day—thinking of things I must remember to tell her or to ask her, expecting to find her sitting reading in her usual place on the sitting-room sofa when I come home; when I'm alone, imagining I hear her voice . . . Grief and loss. Still the thought crosses my mind that I may have contributed to bringing about her end, love her as I did above all else.

The medical history of her illness was long. It began more than two years before the end. It seemed that something was going wrong inside her body. I wanted her to take decisive steps about it—and sensed a curious reluctance, evasiveness . . . It's very difficult to press someone you love to take such steps, impossible to say, 'You must go to a doctor and ask if you've got cancer.' Though a suspicion of it, a sort of precognition of 'the worst', is clearly passing to and fro unspoken between you. When signs appeared of her abdomen beginning to swell (cancer produces an accumulation of fluid), she did take steps—and met with the cause of the swelling being missed not just once but twice. It was by sheer chance that she was seen by a third person who said, 'You must see a surgeon before the end of next week.'

She was admitted under the National Health Service into our nearest hospital, Queen Mary's, Roehampton, on Friday of the following week. Thus began for us two years of alternating hope and fear. (On the preceding Sunday we gave a midday party for about sixty of our friends—without telling them, of course. A great success. A few of them thought she didn't look well.) The first tests of the fluid showed no cancer cells. *Hope!* Then surgery on the first of May. (I have always thought 'April is the cruellest month' was an incredible statement; how can one say that a period of time exercises cruelty? May, though, the month of flowers blooming and birds singing, ever recalls to us the unhappiest of months.) Shortly after the operation the surgeon let me know that he would speak to me when he next visited her on his round; he had already spoken to both of us before the operation, so that we should understand what was going on. They had put my wife to begin with in one of four little glass private wards on either side of a corridor at the end of the gynaecological ward. (It was thought she had an ovarian disturbance.) I waited for him, leaning against the wall outside the corridor, looking down the ward: women lying in beds, flowers on tables, nurses moving about, bright sunlight coming through the windows.

The surgeon came out, recognized me, engaged me with a friendly smile. I was able to put to him the dread question which he must have had to face God knows how many times: 'Was it cancer?' He answered in what affected me strongly as an honest, manly fashion: he thought it was, though there were the results of incidental confirmatory tests still to come in. *Fear* . . . And the second question: 'Were you able to remove it all?' To which he said he couldn't at present be certain; he might want to have another 'look round' inside, after an interval. In the meantime she would be put on to chemotherapy aimed at suppressing anything that might remain. *Hope!*

After a few days my wife was moved into the main ward. She became passionately absorbed in ward-life. In no time at all she knew all the nurses and in scarcely more time the rest of the patients in the ward. She knew them all by their Christian names, and they—plus the kitchen-helps who came round with trolley and served tea and meals—called her by her Christian name. She rapidly learned what the other patients were suffering from and, as soon as she could get around, called on them and chatted to them, made friends . . . How different from me! When later on I had a major hip operation, my inclination was to spend most of my time with the curtains drawn a little—when I had the nerve to draw them—reading books, listening to Radio 3, and chatting to friends who came to see me. True, I couldn't get around to other patients as, being under traction, I was pinned down on my back with a five-pound weight dangling from my foot for three out of the four weeks. (Incidentally I noticed that male patients, although sometimes two of them would get together and talk for hours, did much less miscellaneous chatting than the females.) And, while I called the nurses by their Christian names, the majority of them, after a month, were still calling me mister.

My wife, on the other hand, was in due course comforting and consoling any other women patients who wanted her to. Although she normally read a great deal, much more than I, she began to read less. And such was her absorption in ward-life that when I was with her and recounting a piece of news or describing some incident that affected me, her attention would suddenly flick away, completely caught by something that was happening further down the ward. Irritating! It happened frequently. Yet equally frequently I was confronted by the serious thought that if *sympathique* could properly describe anyone, such a one was my wife.

The second operation to 'look round' inside took place, and the surgeon talked to me about it afterwards. The bulk of the cancer had been excised: he found a certain number of 'seedlings' which he had removed. ('Seedlings'—in one's garden one nurtured them to help them to grow and looked forward to when they would spread out their stems and flower.) There was one relic of the cancer, he said, which it would be too dangerous to excise: this could be, would be, treated by chemotherapy. A sort of *hope!* We—my wife and the girls and I—behaved towards each other in hope of a sort. But thinking about that nucleus which might not be excised I privately felt—and long afterwards I discovered both the girls had privately felt—*fear* of a sort! However things went well and three weeks after the operation my wife was discharged. As the senior consultant in chemotherapy who came to see her at the Roehampton hospital was based at the Westminster, she was transferred there for further treatment. Thus began our trips to and from, and finally coming to an end in, the Westminster.

Things continued to go well. My wife went to the Westminster for a 'chemo' treatment each week, usually coming away during the same day, sometimes staying overnight. We had encouragingly understanding personal sessions with the consultant, an impressively active and knowledgeable man; and a young woman doctor with experience of the drug he was treating my wife with was appointed to watch over her, to check the results of the blood-tests she had each time and to counsel her and me—this young woman doctor became a friend. Nothing that we could think of was overlooked or forgotten. The medical treatment and care that my wife received from the National Health Service seems to me entirely above criticism; and the degree of sympathy and attentiveness that was given to both of us from the staffs of the hospitals, from the most senior of consultants to the most junior of nurses, beyond praise: they were splendid. Somehow, in spite of our private suffering, I recall it as a marvellous human experience.

Things were going very well. My wife was beginning to look well, to eat well, to go out and about with me in London and to revive our previous way of life. It was made quite clear to us by the Westminster consultant that chemotherapy was not being presented as a permanent cure: its function was to arrest the cancer, to inhibit its growth—to stop the 'seedlings' from flowering . . . Be that as it may. She was beginning to look well. *Hope!* (We came to recognize later that she must have been at the start of a period of 'remission': we didn't discuss it as such; I don't recall the word's being used between us. Remission is something that has an end . . .) She was beginning to feel well or so she told us. We decided to celebrate by going on holiday. On holiday one forgets about cancer—almost. A couple of trips to Brighton as a start, to stay in the Old Ship Hotel—at the shortest walking distance from pubs, shops, cinemas: we went to the cinema for the first time in ages, discovered a Thai restaurant. Then we became more adventurous and in late autumn went to Cadiz—to a very fine *parador* beside the sea, an old friend of my wife living in a pretty nearby village: late sunshine and sea breezes, *tapas* galore and fifty-five different kinds of sherry.

Briefly into the Westminster again. The swelling in her abdomen had not gone completely down: it never did, despite fluid being drained away in litres at a time. The chemotherapy was holding. Going to parties and literary dos together, she came across other women who confided that they, too, had suffered from cancer or knew someone who had, and thanks to chemotherapy were still living after five years. Five years: who was to say that five years might not extend like Time itself? *Hope! Hope!* We celebrated the new year (in February) with another large Sunday morning party, at which everyone thought she looked marvellous. We embarked on more holidays, looking for more sunshine and sea breezes: the north coast of Mallorca in June for swimming in the Mediterranean and delicious fresh fish; the Austrian lakes in August, for boat-trips and sumptuous cream-cakes . . . Things were going so well that I could even bear to leave her for a week's writing in a retreat for male 'artists' in Surrey. We were becoming used to remission.

Nineteen eighty-seven ended with occasional trips to the Westminster, and then the requirement for an ultrasound scan. *Fear!* The Roehampton hospital kept in touch, and she was seen by both surgical and gynaecological consultants—they did not abandon their care because she was under a chemotherapy consultant's wing elsewhere. January—more calls to the Westminster with increasing frequency, in and out again, but sometimes in for beyond the usual twenty-four hours. Things were not going well. The remission was drawing to a close. The swelling was back; she was in constant discomfort and finding it difficult to eat. After a longer spell in the Westminster, which we might have taken for the beginning of a spell that was not to end, she was allowed to come home to see how my elder daughter and I could manage: she was confined to bed most of the time. After ten days she felt so ill, was in such discomfort, that we had to call for our doctor, even though it was Sunday—our doctor came, treated her and arranged for an ambulance to carry her back to the Westminster straight away.

Thus began the last weeks. Since the beginning of this term she had been on a saline drip, through which the 'chemo' drug could be administered—a stand beside the bed holding on high a plastic bag from which the liquid flowed down a Perspex tube into a vein in her arm. As she became unable to eat enough to keep her going, a second drip was brought along, from which a nutrient solution flowed down. One stage followed another. *Hope* and *Fear* were dissolved in the face of the *Inevitable* . . .

Throughout these weeks she remained sitting up in bed, stoically, courageously. I visited her every afternoon of the week, with a very occasional afternoon off to attend some literary committee or other. I left home at about two o'clock and got back after six-thirty. (One of the features of sick-visiting someone

185

prolongedly in hospital is coping with day-to-day laundry, taking it away and bringing it back; bringing grapes and flowers is an embellishment on this main function.) When I arrived at her bedside and we had kissed each other, she would look me firmly in the eye and say 'Did you come by taxi?' Woe betide me if I said no.

I have to explain. By this time I was in constant grinding pain from my hip, in which the prosthetic device used to replace the joint ten years earlier had worn out. But while my wife was in hospital I could not countenance the idea of going into hospital myself to have the old prosthetic device replaced by a new one—a much more serious operation than the first, I was told. I went about lamely with a stick. 'You can afford taxis,' my wife would say, no matter how ill she was feeling. It was a regular thing for me to be asked if I had come by taxi, and I couldn't bring myself to lie to her if I had succumbed to the temptation of an Old Age Pensioner's free transport on a bus. And I had to promise to go home by taxi. 'If a bus doesn't come first . . .' I would say.

When I was settled beside her bed I would embark on topics of interest I had prepared in advance, perhaps produce a letter for her to see. As week followed week her interest grew less. She still kept an eye on ward-life and didn't appear to miss anything that was going on. There were moving scenes to be observed: one day a large party, a whole Jewish family, I think, clustered round the bedside of an old man who could not be far off death, weeping copiously. Tears were really rather far from us. I remember only one occasion: thoughtlessly I said to her, 'I shall love you always,' and immediately realized it meant I should go on loving her after she was dead: I burst into tears. Tears came into her eyes . . . 'I love you, I love you,' was all I could whisper. Otherwise we behaved with great restraint, too great for me in one context: sitting beside the bed, in physical pain, tired out, unable to think of any more things to say, I longed just to bend forward and rest my head in her lap. I sometimes did—until she told me that in public, there, it embarrassed her—one of the other women patients had remarked on it.

Sometimes during the afternoon our younger daughter, a free-lance, would join us, perhaps accompanied by the young man she was living with; sometimes in the evening our elder daughter came after work. The two girls occupied themselves gainfully, changing the water for the flowers, scrutinizing the fruit and packing up the next consignment of laundry; then chatting to their mother with much more inspiration than I seemed able to muster. Our younger daughter started up a regular friendly acquaintance with two of the nurses, so as to be able to put to them pertinent questions about her mother's case and its treatment. She kept on till they had answered what she wanted to know; in fact they bore it very well. The upshot was that in the end she knew much more about the case and its treatment than any of us, which was somehow reassuring. And I began to feel that the nurses liked being asked about their work; they had regular little get-togethers with my daughter by the entrance to the ward. Afterwards, the visits seemed to pass slowly, my wife beginning to look too tired for us. (I think she was often too tired for us when we arrived, but the desire to have us there was so strong.) When I was visiting her on my own it would be a relief to me as well as to her when it was time to leave. Having pledged myself to take a taxi 'unless a bus came first . . .' I bought a *Standard* at the bus-stop and then took it to read quietly over a pint of beer in the nearby Pavior's Arms—to read quietly, trying to project myself into a different state of affairs, a different life . . .

To ease the monotony for her, before she was permanently chained to the drips, the hospital suggested she should come home for the weekend. Excitement and trepidation for the girls and me. It happened three times. On the first she was so unwell that it was not a success; on the third she became so ill that we had to telephone for an ambulance on the second day. On the middle one she was feeling a little better and in fairer spirits. She came into the flat, a top-floor flat with the evening sun shining in and exclaimed, 'Doesn't it look pretty!' Her own flat, which she herself had made to look pretty. I wondered—was she wondering, too?—if this was the last time she would ever see it. Actually she did see it, on the third weekend, but was too ill to notice or care.

And so we came to the *Inevitable* . . . I can't recall exactly at what point she said, 'I don't want to leave you all. It's so soon.' Perhaps in between two of the weekends at home or perhaps after the third one. In any case, the way in which her interest in us faded when we were with her, sometimes after no more than ten minutes or so, had made both the girls begin to feel that somehow she was already leaving us. For my part, it invested me with a curious numbness, a sense of remoteness, as if all this were happening behind a window of plate-glass which separated me from it.

Then one day we got a message from the hospital that she wanted to see all three of us together. We met in the foyer of the hospital, and as we entered the ward a nurse—we knew all the nurses ourselves by now—was waiting for us. She said, 'Your wife says she wants to have a heavy talk with you.' 'Heavy' was not one of my wife's words, but the message was ominously clear. When we were gathered around the bed, she addressed us.

'I've told them to cut off the nutrient drip.' She paused a moment and then added with the emphasis of finality, 'It's *my decision*.'

None of us said a word. It was indeed final. Without the nutrient she would not survive. Of course we understood. She was already suffering intolerable discomfort, if not desolating pain. She could eat nothing and was so weak that she could no longer be got out of bed—with all the physical humiliation which that entailed. And of course there was no other outcome than the one she had decided to take immediately. In reply to her none of us said anything.

She then began to tell us the things she wanted us to do after she was dead. (She had left an explicit and orderly will about what was to become of her property, including instructions that she was to be cremated 'at the minimum cost'—we had all agreed to the latter at the time, but regretted it after it happened.) What she intended to talk about now was how she wanted her disposable minor property to be distributed. The fact that there was something she was determined to say seemed to give her an unusual sense of energy. She came to the obsequies. 'You'll have to have all my family,' she said with wry humour—all the family I have is one sister in Philadelphia. 'You'll have to give them something to eat afterwards. Get them some sandwiches from Marks and Spencer's!' It was difficult to believe all this was happening, this matter-of-fact discussion of trivialities. Like much that had gone on during the last few days it had an air of unreality. The 'heavy' talk over, we were at a complete loss for conversation. It was past six o'clock, the time when we usually prepared to leave, when she was more than ready for us to leave. The light of a May evening was fading from the ward, whose grey walls were never inspiringly bright. My wife had said everything. She lay back, exhausted. There was nothing for us to do but leave.

On the way out we spoke to one of the two nurses, asking for a promise that as soon as the end was in sight they would send for us. They promised. They understood; when the end came we were to be *there*, holding her . . . None of us asked the question, 'How long is it likely to be?' They wouldn't have been able to tell us. It was a Friday evening, now. Which day would it be?

We all went to the hospital on the Saturday afternoon and then the Sunday afternoon, sitting quietly round the bed in a sort of vigil. My wife was aware that we were there and that time was passing. At the end of visiting-time on the Sunday afternoon she managed to address the girls, in a kindly tone of voice—'You can go . . .' They gathered themselves together and after lingering embraces left.

I, it appeared, was meant to stay. I stayed another hour, exhausted, reduced. As I left I reminded the nurses of their promise, though I didn't need to. They were so kind. When I got outside I was powerfully called by the Pavior's Arms—I longed for a stiff whisky. But I thought I'd better not as my elder daughter would have prepared our supper. A taxi came up and I got into it.

The taxi drove me home at speed. When I let myself into the flat my elder daughter was waiting for me. 'The hospital has just rung up. Mummy's much worse.'

'We must go,' I said unnecessarily.

'Yes.'

She had telephoned her sister. We called a mini-cab and in a few minutes I was speeding back—thank goodness I hadn't gone to the Pavior's Arms!—in the direction from which I had just come.

We all met down below in the foyer of the hospital. My younger daughter's young man had come with her: the four of us went up to the ward, where the two nurses on night duty were waiting for us. The lights were out and everywhere was silent. We were led to my wife's bed, where the curtains were drawn. We sat in chairs close to the bed. I sat nearest to my wife's head and took hold of her hand:

189

the two girls on either side behind me took hold of her. We think she knew we were there. She was lying on her side, her face sweating and distorted, her hair damp and awry, the sheets rumpled. She was breathing stertorously in violent gasps—a racking sound. From time to time she squeezed my fingers. I couldn't tell if it was a voluntary effort to convey a message or an involuntary spasm. Each of us whispered to her, 'I'm *here* . . .'

She was fighting for breath, fighting to live, perhaps fighting not to leave us. So soon . . . It was agonizing to watch, but all three of us holding her were under control. After a little while a young woman doctor whom we hadn't seen before came in. Tentatively, with great tact, she put it to us: Would we like her to give my wife an injection to ease her on her way out?

'Oh, please *do*!'

The doctor gave her the injection. We went on holding her; the stertorous gasps went on without perceptible diminution. The agony persisted.

The doctor came again, with a second offer. 'Oh, *please* do!' Still it persisted.

At last a third time. We went on holding her, our most loved one. And the gasps stopped. I thought she must have died and I closed her eyelids. The gasps started again, but only for a minute or so, and then they stopped . . . I pressed my finger gently down her eyelids for the last time. It was over.

The doctor looked in, then the nurses. The girls and I stood up and clung to each other, weeping—for I don't know how long. My younger daughter's young man stood waiting for her. At one moment my elder daughter leaned her head back from my shoulder so as to look at me—'We will look after *you*!' At last it was time to give up. The nurses were waiting outside the curtains. They came in with a question: Would we like a cup of tea?

In fact the idea was that, while we were drinking a cup of tea, they, the nurses, would make my wife look tidier for our last sight of her. So we sat, the four of us, in the nurses' little room off the end of the ward, where they had a tray with cups and tea-bags and an electric kettle boiling. We found it a very acceptable cup of tea. It was the early hours of Monday morning.

We were led back and shown through the curtains one at a

time. The apparatus of the drips, the stands, the Perspex tubes and the plastic bags had been swept away. My wife was still lying on her side, but her face had been wiped and her hair combed. I looked at her—stunned. She had never had many lines on her face, just a few down her upper lip. Now every trace of life's storms had gone. She looked simply *beautiful* . . .

I bent down and kissed her cheek for the last time: to my lips it felt as smooth and fresh as it did on the day I married her, thirty-eight years ago.

I waited while the girls took their last turn with their mother, and then with our arms around each other we walked out, down the stairs and out of the hospital. My younger daughter's young man had been getting taxis for us. One for her and himself, to take them back to their home. One last kiss to the girls, then my elder daughter helped me into the other taxi, to take us back to our home.

GRANTA 9: JOHN BERGER
BORIS

Also
THE SOLITUDE OF LATIN AMERICA

- Gabriel García Márquez

- Mario Vargas Llosa

- Patrick Marnham

- Don McCullin

- José Donoso

- Manlio Argueta

Plus
Russell Hoban,
Graham Swift,
T. Coraghessan Boyle,
James Wolcott and others.

'An extraordinary story of love and greed.'
<u>New Society</u>

 Granta 9 is again available at £5.00 from
Granta, FREEPOST, Cambridge CB1 1BR.

RUDOLF SCHÄFER
DEAD FACES

Rudolf Schäfer

Photographing the dead is not new—in the last century, it was quite common—but people do find the idea rather strange. Many people today don't know what a dead person looks like. In modern society we are separated from the event of death: somebody becomes ill and goes into hospital, and then there's a phone call or a telegram informing you of the death, and the body is prepared and put in the coffin, and the coffin is put in the grave and that's it. There is no direct experience of what death actually looks like, and people have formed this notion that it must look terrible because the events leading to it were terrible.

These photographs may also seem strange merely because of the way I've presented them. A full-face portrait, perfectly natural in life, seems unnatural in death. These are ordinary poses. We are constantly bombarded with newspaper and television pictures of catastrophes and wars—violent, extreme pictures—but we defuse one of the implications of these images—our own mortality—with the thought that nothing so extreme will ever happen to us. With these pictures you simply don't have that option.

They were all taken in the Pathological Institute of the Charité—an old university clinic here in Berlin. It was not particularly difficult to get permission: sometimes I obtained the consent of the relatives; in other cases that wasn't necessary. Of the dead themselves I knew only a few details: when they were born, when they died, what they died of. Nothing more. These people all died of natural causes. People remark that they all look very peaceful. That is the point: there is nothing special about these faces. The peace of this moment, this coming to rest: this is what dead people look like.

Even so, some people react with moral outrage: how could I rob these people of their last remaining possession, their dignity? They have a point and I'm not denying that the moral dilemma exists, but you have to reach beyond it to see what is perhaps more important, namely, the questions the pictures raise in our own minds about ourselves. To me the pictures have a terrible beauty; they are beautiful. At the same time, the question they pose cannot be avoided. The one thing I think I learned during this period is that life is too short to waste on unimportant things. These pictures show what will surely become of us all one day, and we should therefore take a little bit more care over our lives.

Interview conducted and translated from the German by Piers Spence.

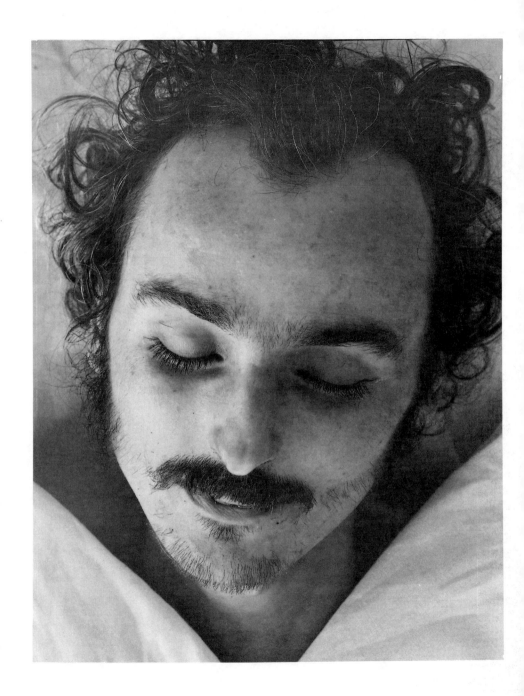

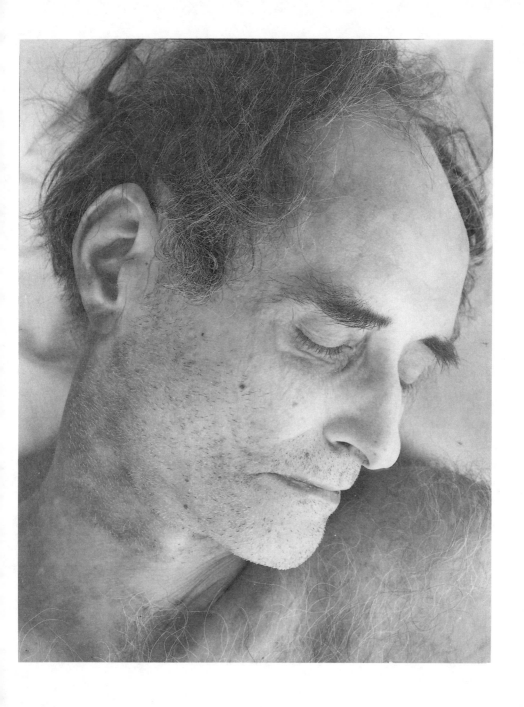

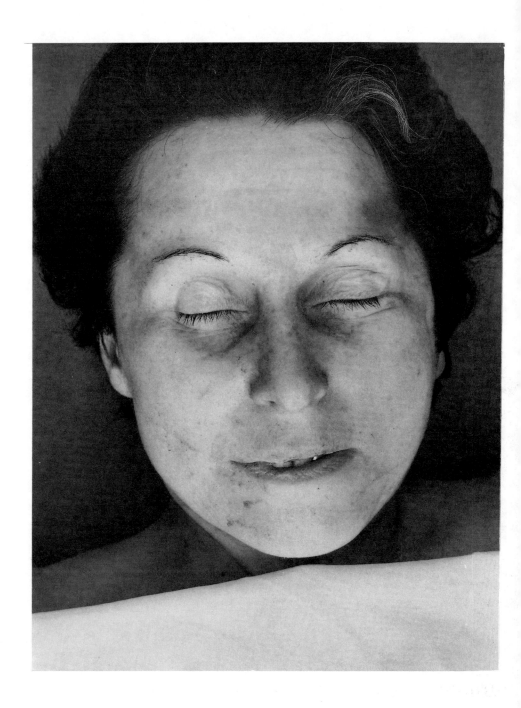

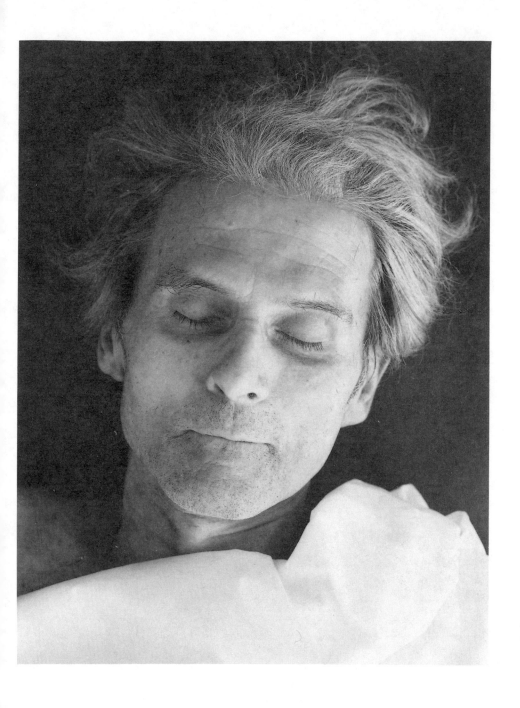

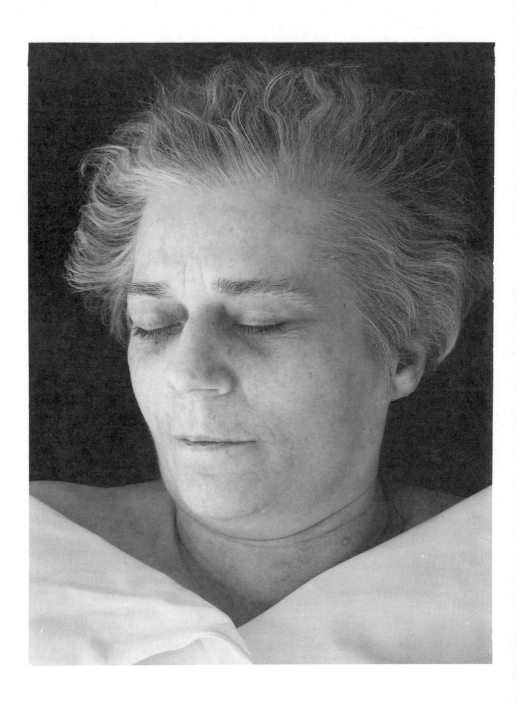

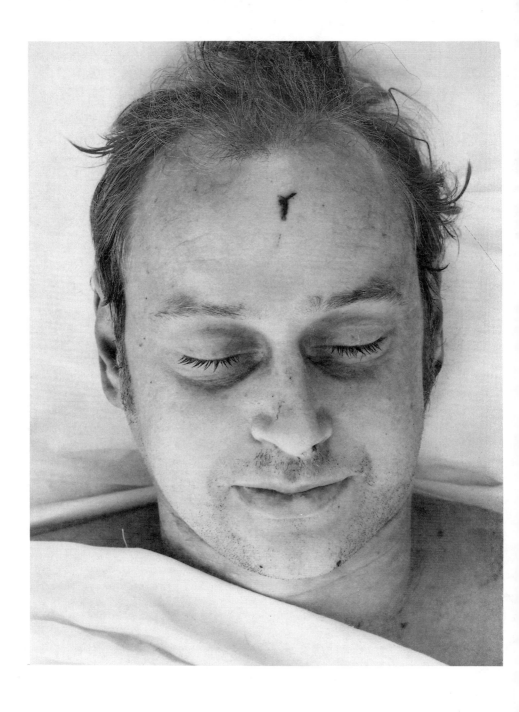

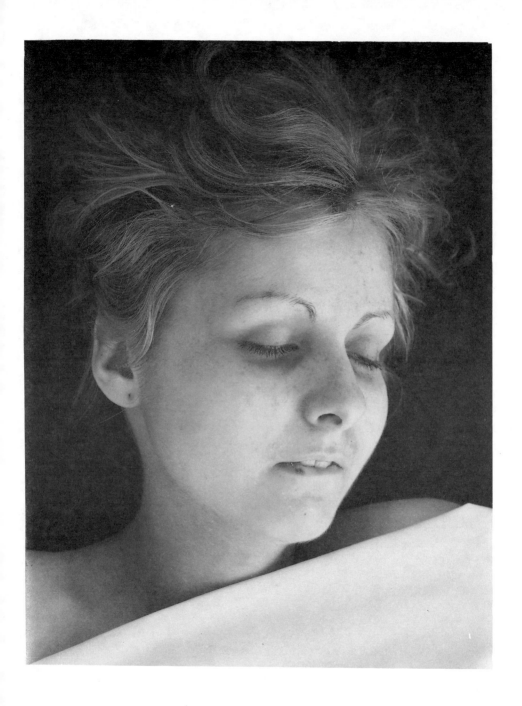

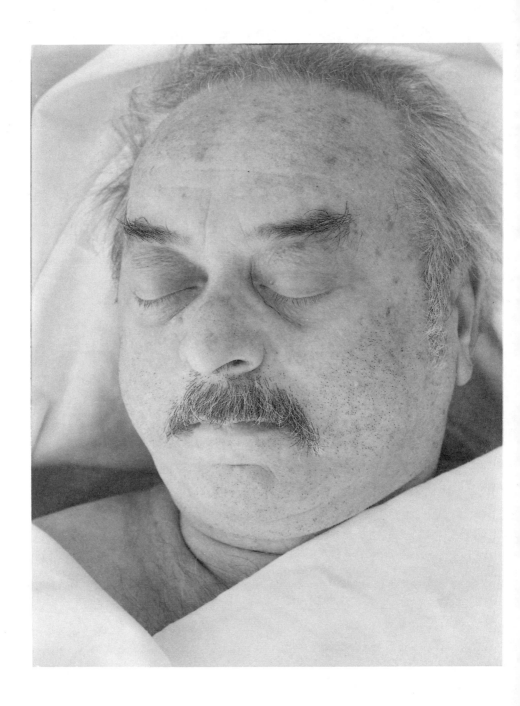

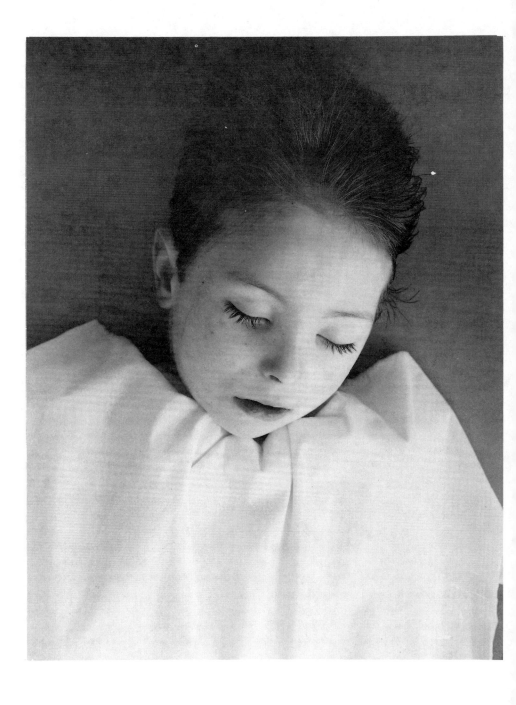

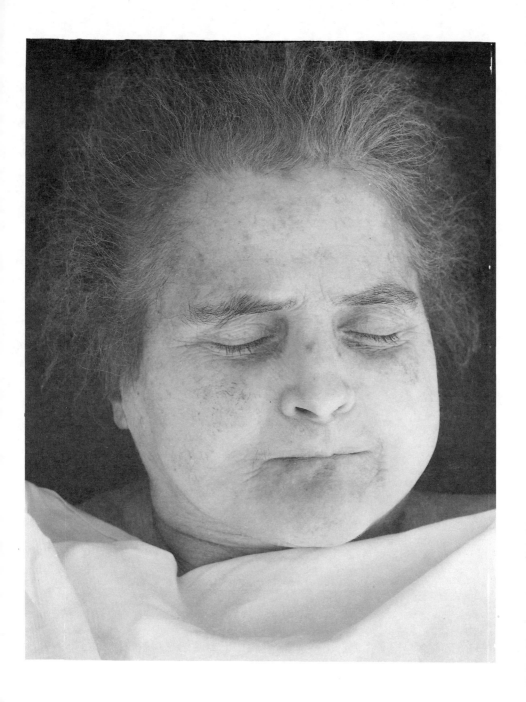

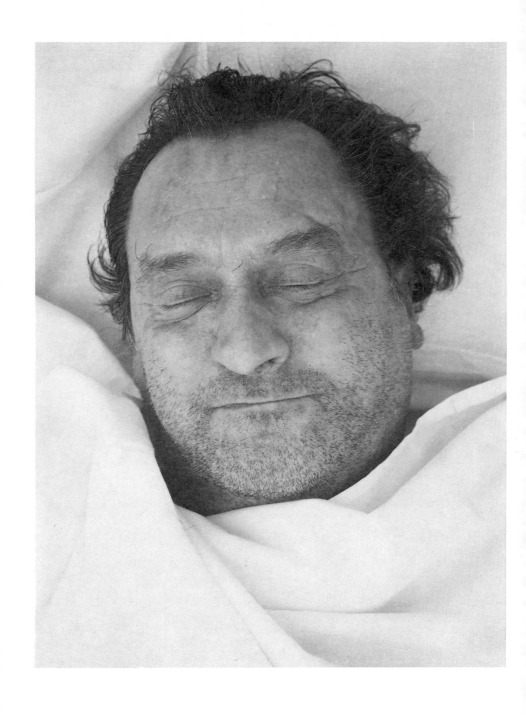

CHRISTOPHER PETIT
ROBINSON

There was something vaguely familiar about Robinson. Long after we became friends I remembered I had seen him once before in a pub called the Angel, standing at the bar with another man. I had been struck by his air of persuasion and watched him out of idle curiosity while waiting for a woman who was late. Robinson physically dominated the conversation. I thought he would overstep the mark, but his positioning was faultless. The other man nodded a lot and had on a dark jacket, I remember, because once Robinson, without interrupting himself, leaned over and brushed something from the lapel.

Had I not subsequently met Robinson I would have forgotten the incident (and did until much later anyway). Looking back, I remembered his intimacy and the fact that he was standing, while with me he made a point of sitting. I could not help notice the white cap he wore. It had made me dislike him hugely on sight.

From what I gathered later, Robinson had taken great care to invent himself. He was tall and boyish, with his hair swept back: like Orson Welles as Harry Lime in *The Third Man*, that same moon face. He cultivated the resemblance, and I fancied I saw in the high shine of his toe-caps a vain reminder of that introduction to Lime: 'EXT. VIENNA NIGHT—Close-up, black Oxfords in dark doorway.' Sometimes too he addressed me with a mocking 'Old man'.

His voice, his way of speaking, was his most arresting quality. It was a centred voice. He knew its value and exploited it. It was not accent or fluency that gave it charm, but pitch. Robinson knew by instinct what note to adopt. His was the most confidential voice I had ever heard. The telephone was always his best medium. To me, at least, he'd just say, 'How're you?' or 'How're things?' without introducing himself, knowing I'd know who it was. He used the telephone cunningly and knew that ground could be gained where it wouldn't face to face. Sometimes during a call he'd call me Christo, which no one had done since I was a child.

Our relationship depended on a dozen or so public places of Robinson's choosing. If I suggested one pub he'd say another. If I said seven-thirty he'd say, 'Can we make it twenty minutes later?' Then he would add as an afterthought, 'Old

Photo: David Hurn (Magnum)

man. You don't mind?' Such fine tuning of the social itinerary was typical of him, and I never did mind, much. Robinson liked the Wheatsheaf, north of Oxford Street, the gloomy Admiral Duncan and the De Hems on the border of Soho's Chinatown, when it was still seedy and full of Chinese. The De Hems was temporarily closed following a stabbing which Robinson had witnessed. The victim had died before his eyes, and Robinson described these last moments with a clinical reverence while I imagined him, taller than the rest, leaning forward with his characteristic stare, not flinching from the punctured throat, frothing with pink bubbles, or from the dying man's milky gaze.

Even then, I was intrigued by Robinson, more so in fact than when we first met on the corner of Manette Street one evening as night fell. Almost immediately we lost the person who had introduced us, a feckless and charming young man in the film business who was always double- or triple-booked and spent his whole life trying to catch up. Robinson cocked his head towards the arch at the end of the street to see if I was going in his direction. I nodded and we fell into step.

We passed into Greek Street under the archway that was to become our favourite entrance to the area because it was like a border-post, the crossing-point where obligations could be left behind.

We turned left. Robinson talked about how one had to look hard to find the remains of the shivering, naked heart of the city that Soho had once been: the countless creaking, winding stairs leading to poky rooms, the ascendant lured on by whatever clumsy enticement was offered by the crudely hand-lettered card stuck next to the downstairs bell. On that first evening we collided with a man ducking out after his swift transaction upstairs, already moving at street speed as he came through the door.

Robinson stopped and peered at the whore's card by the bell. Written in pathetic, childish capitals was the name Monique. He looked at me. 'Do you fancy going up?'

'Not particularly.'

'Did you ever go to a whore?'

I felt a flash of irritation at this importuning, and Robinson let me see that he knew I'd been drawn. 'Oh, I'm curious, that's all,' he said lightly; eye contact, smile. His smile was frank and I decided to like him after all and to go along with whatever the evening might bring.

He started to stroll on. 'I'm all in favour of the financial transaction myself. How many fucks, do you reckon, in the history of Soho?' He speculated on the matter the length of Greek Street. 'Ah, the statistics of sexual activity,' he said at one point. 'Was there ever a second in the history of this district when one couple or another wasn't?' Robinson continued, deep in his own burrowing. It took me a while to learn how his mind worked, in loops, and that his monologues fizzed and sparked before suddenly burning themselves out, as this one did, about half-way down Old Compton Street. Robinson was staring at his shiny toe-caps.

'Here! All around us,' he said quietly, addressing me as though I were backward, and gestured with his head up at the lighted windows above. 'Go to the suburbs and take a look at the houses at night and you know nothing's going on. Am I right?'

He made the question sound both rhetorical and uncomfortably personal. One of the windows went dark and a few doors down another lit up. Smart young couples drifted past, up from the suburbs for a night out. Robinson saw my hesitation.

'A married man, I'll bet,' he said.

I shrugged.

'Ah, fuck your wife!' he said and walked off.

I watched his departing back, the sway of his elegant coat. The click of his shoes: metal quarters on the heels, I decided. The ambiguity of the insult was clever, and, now that I know him better, I can see that it was calculated. At the time, I felt I could take or leave such smart talk. Then Robinson stopped and walked back to me. He had a little aluminium container in his hand and was shaking something from it, a pill he slipped into his mouth. This sneaky little sequence was performed with great dexterity, like a conjuring trick done to test my observation. Robinson smiled ruefully and apologized for his rudeness.

2

Robinson was not of the suburbs. He lived in the middle of town and usually went on somewhere after I'd jacked it in and gone home.

If I missed the last tube, I sometimes had a hard time finding a taxi prepared to drive out so far, and then I'd often be short of cash and have to search the house for spare change while the knocking diesel engine of a waiting cab started to wake the street. A few times I borrowed off Robinson, who always carried a fat wad in his back pocket, held in a money-clip. The clip had a ruby embedded in it, unusually flashy for him.

One night, I wound up in Oxford Street, drunk and without money. I returned to where Robinson had been but he had moved on. I got caught in a summer storm, so rather than get completely soaked I ran to the office to wait there for it to pass. I fell asleep without meaning to and when I awoke it was already light.

The office belonged to a small film company run by a handful of wide-boys who employed a number of molls whom they passed around among themselves. These young men liked to be thought of as wolves: hand carelessly over the telephone mouthpiece—caller hanging on—instructions shouted through the open door to the secretary to tell the next caller to fuck off, then sweetly into the receiver, 'Not you, John.' Feet were swung on to the desk, the phone cradled lovingly into the neck and a grin fixed in place (they all grinned on the phone, always). Conversation started with some fresh morsel of social gossip, a patter that could go on for twenty minutes before business was mentioned. Then the distinguishing features became a mixture of jargon, flirtation—'If we're going to get into bed together,' was a fashionable office cliché that summer—and cheerful aggression: 'Do us a favour, go on, fuck off.' They necked casually in the office with the molls and, if anyone came into the room, they said things like, 'Excuse me if I don't stand up, I've got a hard-on.' Robinson called them the condom-in-the-wallet boys.

After work they went around in a pack, drinking in pubs and furiously arguing over business they were too disorganized to fit

Photo (preceding pages): Laurie Sparham (Network)

into the day, though they always appeared busy, unlike myself. They infuriated me: their passionate squabbling, their nursery mentality, their effortless spiel and self-aggrandizement, their involvement, the bits of power-play, quite byzantine in their sloppy elaborateness. I was jealous. My own career was becalmed and my nerve not holding, which was why I had exchanged free-lancing for a dubious executive status.

I re-read Fitzgerald's *The Crack-up* travelling in and out on the underground. I told myself, not without satisfaction, that I'd burned out before my time. There was even a sense of achievement in this, a compensation for a larger failure. (I had nothing much to my name—a handful of scripts, more often filmed than not, none as good as I'd once thought.) I was drawn to emulate Fitzgerald's crash, though realizing, not enough of the time, that I'd done nothing to earn it. Either way, I found myself not putting up with things in the way I once did.

I discovered I liked the quiet and the white of the office when no one was there. During the mild nights of midsummer I took to sleeping on a piece of flat roof, in a sleeping-bag bought for the purpose. The office was down a quiet mews through a low archway under which derelicts drank cider and sweet sherry. The building was a former sweat-shop and probably stables before that. My own office had only a skylight, and the absence of windows lent a mood of detention to each day. The rest of the place was a warren of stairs, rooms within rooms and crooked corridors. One day by accident I found a disused flight of stairs that led up to a set of attic rooms, empty and covered with dust, unused for years, apparently, except by pigeons, mice and rats. The walls had faded from, at a guess, cream to something the colour of the North Sea on a rough day. There was an old toilet that still worked and a basin that ran cold water. The bare wood floors were still littered with buttons dropped by seamstresses. They crunched underfoot and sparkled in moonlight. When the weather was bad I dragged the sleeping-bag in there and listened to the rain and the occasional shout or smash of an empty bottle from the derelicts under the arch.

There were mornings when I failed to come round before others arrived for work, and then I was woken by a telephone

ringing somewhere or the clack-clack of the photocopy machine directly below. Other mornings I wouldn't show up at all. I said I was at meetings and started to fabricate schedules in advance: my office diary became a log-book of appointments that would never take place. There was plenty to occupy me during these slow, hung-over mornings. My drinking had become indiscriminate, and attempts to retrace the voyage of the night before invariably faltered because gaps were starting to appear—great white spaces like white spaces on a map. At first the discovery of these white spaces was disconcerting, but I learned to see in them a not unpleasant sense of mystery. With practice I learned to make the extra effort to note, in the course of an evening's degeneration, a handful of signs for later: a look, a phrase, the arrival of a fresh drink or a remark made to a waiter. All could act as possible markers, as though establishing a criminal alibi.

There was a song on a juke-box in one of the places where Robinson and I drank that began, *It was fun for a while*, which was how I felt about my double life. The professional side of it was, by now, completely shot. I was responsible, though how responsible I could never decide, for sorting out and editing a script while money was raised for a production that was always going to begin in six weeks. 'Everyone wants to do business with us,' I was told with the phoney sincerity that was the company trademark. Sorting out the script meant telling the writers that every clever idea they put in was too expensive and would have to go. There were long discussions with various technical experts about whether a diabolical little creature that resembled an ordinary doll was going to be a remote-controlled dummy—and therefore the responsibility of a special effects team—or a midget in some sort of disguise, in which case it would fall under the category of prosthetics and make-up. Nobody could decide. Artists were hired to make drawings, and still no one could make up their minds. Prosthetics experts, usually earnest young men, were ushered in and asked to speculate upon how this creature might best manifest itself.

    Robinson quizzed me incessantly about these dreary, humourless meetings, which he then related to others, making

Photo (preceding pages): David Hurn (Magnum)

them sound like hours of knockabout fun. Fascinated by these ingenious bores, he asked me bring one to the pub, but when I did Robinson lasted ten minutes of drone before downing his drink and making his excuses.

I found I was spending more and more evenings drinking with Robinson. Perhaps it was because he was capable of interpreting my frustrations in his humorous way. He also moved with an attractive crowd, easy-going, smart and attended by apparently available women who probably credited me with having a more influential address book than was the case.

Then I got fired, or rather I left before getting fired. The anticipated production delay was now a fact because one part of the finance had fallen through. Recrimination was in the air: blame the script, whose fault, fire accordingly. New writers would be found, and further scapegoats hired. I was tired of the false deadlines, the artificial panics, so many speculative meetings, too much lying. The script wouldn't be ready on the first day of shooting—if there ever were such a thing—because now the film was having to be done on the cheap and the budget had been shaved. There would be cuts and revisions right up until the end of filming. The whole thing was as rickety as a house of cards. I went for a walk one afternoon and didn't go back.

The film did get made and flopped, so I had a last laugh and the satisfaction of handing to an ambitious rival enough rope to hang himself. This he duly did a year or so later, both more spectacularly and more literally than I ever could have anticipated. I went to the funeral.

3

I carried on spending time in Soho and did not tell anyone what I had done, not even Robinson, sometimes meeting people for lunch, as though everything were normal. I started the mornings at the Bar Italia: *espressi* taken standing at the zinc counter, while in the background on a huge video screen Italy versus Brazil, and the Rossi goals that took the *azzuri* to the World Cup Final, were

replayed for the millionth time. I tried to remember to have a spot to eat. Bookshops were good for passing time, then a couple of drinks while reading the paper cover to cover and the luxury of being able to sit in a deserted pub so early after morning opening. For lunch I met acquaintances with expense accounts (avoiding those in the film business) and made it the main meal of the day—got to keep the stomach lined on these jags—drinking white wine, saving the red for evening.

I found it hard to leave the area. It felt as though I'd be breaking a spell. Even when lunch was spun out until three and later, it was tiring wandering about, waiting for evening, so I started napping for an hour or two in one of the cinemas. Soho cinemas showed nothing except porno films. There was no other sort in the area, apart from the private preview theatres of the film trade.

The porno cinemas were well behind what Robinson called the skirting-board of society. To stand in the gloom of the entrance of the auditorium, eyes adjusting to the dark, was to become slowly aware of a picture of magnificent furtiveness: upturned faces, pale and as hushed and expectant as communicants at an altar-rail. And the cinema always full, not half-empty as you might expect. So many of us down there, was my first impression; middle-aged men for the most part, nearly all white and white-collar. The films were foreign and full of badly dubbed grunts. The actors went through the motions with an air of detachment, and the women, in the act of spreading themselves, appeared to retreat beyond reach into private reverie. Sometimes the whole audience tossed and swayed as though bucketed by a tempest, and the seats creaked louder than the sound-track.

Then I saw the voyeur. I only noticed him because he was in my line of vision when I woke up. From the front row he watched the others as they watched the screen. He wore a cap and the lenses from his little round spectacles caught light from the projector. He lifted a bottle, or so I thought. Then I realized they were field-glasses. The voyeur was using field-glasses to study the audience.

I saw him several times, always sitting in the front row. I know he saw me, and I half-expected to see him in the street for I would

Photos (preceding pages): Laurie Sparham (Network)

have known him at once, even though I'd never seen him in the light. Once I saw him with Robinson, but I decided later that it must have been a dream. I never mentioned the porno cinemas to Robinson. Part of me mistrusted him, even then.

Robinson was usually in the Blue Posts soon after five-thirty, sitting upstairs in the lounge bar that was a left-over from the fifties, in front of him the gin he took to set himself up for the evening. He liked to observe the ebb and flow of the first couple of hours after opening. First, the hurried drinks taken straight after work by office types, who downed their glasses in quick succession, blew their resolutions to go by seven and left loudly and uncertainly between forty to fifty minutes later, their hangovers due to set in before the end of the evening unless of course they contined drinking at home. Then came the arrival of those who had gone home, changed and come back to make a night of it. Robinson could calculate the exact duration of the hiatus, usually no more than twenty minutes, between the two squashes. Once he looked at me and asked, 'Are you all right? Old man.' I was able to shrug off the question. I had a summer cold I caught off Robinson and was able to blame that.

When we found ourselves foot-loose at the end of a night, we would idly follow people for a few blocks to see where they went, betting on which way they would turn. Then we started shadowing drunks. The drunker they were the more Robinson appeared to enjoy himself. Staggering couples weaved their uncertain way, cannoning off each other and back, then falling into dark doorways where they clung to each other, fumbling, helpless, suddenly fidgety with lust. At this point, Robinson would leave them to it, rather to my surprise. I was usually drunk enough to want only to stay where I was. Sober, I felt bad about these nocturnal wanderings, following those more helpless than myself (I wondered if this were not part of some strategy of Robinson's), though secretly, at the time, I enjoyed the vicarious power these vignettes of incapacity gave. The logic I used to continue these excursions was that Robinson had to be accompanied because his enormous violence was held in check only by my restraining presence. I'd not seen this violence yet, but knew it was there. Once in one of the alleys connecting Wardour and Dean Streets we came across a man passed out in a doorway, a man in a suit, not a derelict. Robinson bet me that I didn't have the nerve to roll him. 'You'd like to but you daren't,' he said.

Sometimes Robinson approached the drunks. He'd ask for a cigarette and scrounge one and light for both of them, hands cupped carefully around the flame of an old Dunhill lighter he carried, though he did not smoke. (The cigarettes were always passed on to me.) Not until he'd produced the Dunhill a number of times did it strike me how little Robinson carried in the way of personal possessions. The money-clip, the little aluminium container of pills (one of which he took from time to time) and the lighter were all I'd seen. I assumed the lighter was of sentimental value, but Robinson said he had found it. I doubted this since there was so much he chose not to carry: no watch, no address book, no scraps of paper, no cheque-books, no credit cards, none of the junk or bits of identification that most people accumulate. One evening Robinson sifted idly through my own wallet and found more than twenty samples of my signature on bank and credit cards and their receipts, two passport-size photographs of myself, a driving-licence that I had forgotten to sign, two other records of my address and various scraps of paper with telephone numbers scribbled on them. Robinson asked who the numbers belonged to and I couldn't remember.

It must have occurred to me that I knew next to nothing about Robinson, but somehow that seemed not to be the point. Robinson was a constant fact at a time when everyone else was uncertain: the reliable drinking companion. Any misgivings I had—and there were plenty swarming just below the surface— I suppressed or forgot in alcohol. When my own wrist-watch stopped I didn't bother to wind it again, a little act of self-consciousness that I saw as a symbol of my present condition. I'd let everything run down, then start over again. It was a time full of resolutions, and, in drink, a buzzing articulacy that never found expression in words.

Photo: Laurie Sparham (Network)

Christopher Petit

One afternoon I woke up in a porno cinema with no memory of getting there. I had to use the toilet and pushed my way down the row, past grumbling customers (a scene was reaching noisy climax on the sound-track). The walk to the toilet made me see how drunk I was, not hopeless but walking an awkward path close to an unseen drop. Two exit signs over the door, shut one eye and the two slid into one—in the land of the blind—a final falsetto scream from the sound-track, and the whole cinema fell quiet, apart from late-comers. I barged through the toilet door. There was someone already in there, and I avoided standing right by him, went to the next urinal but one and reminded myself not to be careless because of the drink and spray my shoes, but the urinals were the bowl sort fixed to the wall, which made it easier.

The other man was just standing there, not pissing at all by the sound of it. I splashed about with a worldly air, stuffed my free hand in my pocket and said to myself that I didn't know a man that didn't sneak a look at the man standing next to him in a public toilet. I glanced out of the corner of my eye and the sight made no sense, even taking into account looking askance and double vision from drink: two of them standing at the same urinal. I looked a bit more: definitely two people, one tiny though, it seemed, being held up by the other so his feet rested on the rim of the urinal. A child in a porno cinema toilet? I splashed at the sugar cubes of disinfectant in the urinal (a dainty touch, I thought, considering the nature of the establishment). There were surreptitious movements to my right. I could guess what they were up to. I should finish up and get out, but I didn't. I stared at the sugar cubes pitted where I'd pissed on them, watched them floating when the urinal flushed itself. I stood there, drunk, finished with pissing, fly undone, waiting to see if I became aroused. I wondered if, as well as catching a cold off Robinson, he had passed on something else: a clinical inquisitiveness, akin to a virus, that made the contemplation of anything permissible. The shock was not in the discovery but in my own, suddenly alert curiosity.

Then the child—Christ, what was I doing, standing there?—turned his head. I saw the flash of light in the little round lenses. It was the voyeur. I could not grasp the transformation. Then I saw:

Photo (preceding pages): Laurie Sparham (Network)

232

the voyeur was not a child—not some angel with the eyes of a sewer rat—but a forty-year-old dwarf. He smiled mirthlessly, and in a lurch of puddled logic I remembered dreary discussions about how to make some diabolical little movie monster convincing, and here was the answer, and then I remembered none of that mattered any more. I fled, I know, and must have gone back to the auditorium and hidden in the middle of a row (I was not in a state to face the streets) and passed out. That's where I came to, at any rate.

R obinson was in a vile mood that evening. I had sobered up drinking tomato juice for Bloody Mary whenever it was my round and was spoiling for a fight. Then I drank too much in the half-hour before closing and was drunk again. I'd tried to draw Robinson out, to get him to answer questions about himself, such as where his money came from (another fat roll I saw that night) and why he never carried anything of note, but he was having none of it and for a while went off to talk to someone else down the other end of the bar. I sat there helpless, incapable of decision, protected by the dull noise of the pub. We were in the De Hems, where there had been the stabbing. It was nicely done out now, more like a singles bar. I looked carefully at the women.

'Do you fancy her?' Robinson asked when he came back and found me staring at a tall woman who looked bored and drunk. The man with her was as drunk, and by then everyone else in the pub was too. Robinson seemed cheered up. I'd forgotten what our quarrel was about and was quite happy to go along with whatever he suggested.

We ended up following the drunk couple. The cool night air made them even more light-headed and helpless as they tottered down Greek Street. I missed my footing once or twice but was still capable of imitating someone more sober than myself. Robinson was virtually silent.

Twenty or thirty yards ahead of us, they turned right into Manette Street (where Robinson and I had first met). We walked through the arch to find the man vomiting copiously over some railings, and the woman flat on the pavement, skirt ridden up over her knees, one shoe dangling, eyes fluttering like demented moths. The man dry-heaved, a prelude to a second bout of vomiting. As his buttocks clenched with every spasm, the wallet in his hip pocket nudged itself into view. It was there for the taking, as was the woman whose puppet-like display now extended to thighs and suspender belt. The symmetry of the components and their utter defencelessness were an open invitation to dramatic intervention. Robinson was taking command, and I found myself urgently wanting to crack the vomiting man's teeth with my shoe, to catch him full force as he bowed to retch, snapping his head back so that the puke shot from his mouth in a backward arc. Jesus, aren't I the fucking dandy? Robinson was helping the woman to her feet, and ordered me to find a cab. Ah, fuck you too, I thought, and slouched off to the end of the street, but there weren't any in the Charing Cross Road just then. One with its light on didn't stop. Manette Street was empty when I got back. Where the fuck were they? Robinson and the woman had done a bunk. I didn't see the man at first, but he was still clinging on to the railings, a miserable sight with vomit down him, eyes swimming behind his glasses. The wallet had dropped to the pavement. I picked it up. He had his glasses off now which gave him that sleepy, vulnerable look some people get when they remove their spectacles. I asked where Robinson and the woman were, but he could not make sense of the question. He managed to fold his glasses all right. It took a long time. When he tried to put them in his shirt pocket, he kept snagging the top of the pocket and missing. He snorted and looked helpless. I told him to look up at the stars, it'd make him feel better and, as he did, he suddenly sat down on his arse with a bump and looked so surprised I didn't have the gall to kick him in the mouth as I'd promised myself. I wanted to stamp on his spectacles, which were lying on the ground. Instead I picked them up and stuffed them in his top pocket.

4

I was going to post the wallet back the next day when I remembered what I had in mind, and hung on to it.

The next time I saw Robinson he was with the couple from Manette Street, which made me feel a bit queasy. I was about to slip off when Robinson spotted me and made introductions. The man blinked behind his glasses and showed no sign of recognition. We shook hands, and Robinson looked smug as though he had brought us together for some purpose. I wondered if the whole thing had been a set-up. I half expected him to put his hand deftly into my pocket and produce the other man's wallet and return it as though completing a conjuring trick. He'd had the woman, of that I had no doubt.

The man with glasses and the woman were not a couple as I had thought, so he didn't care half as much as I did that she had gone off with Robinson. I suspected that Robinson and the woman's version of what happened—that the man had said he'd find his own way when he felt well enough to move—was probably not accurate. I was sure they had dumped him. Robinson and the woman went around together for a while.

I liked the way I contrived to pass the wallet on to Robinson. I transferred the contents to my own wallet, and one evening in a pub casually dropped the stolen one where Robinson was bound to notice. Eventually I picked it up and asked if it was his. He replied that he didn't have one (as I suspected). I pressed him to take it. The gesture was intended as a back-handed joke since Robinson never carried anything to put in a wallet. It felt right, the idea of him carrying an empty wallet. Perhaps he suspected where it had come from, and that I'd given it to him partly in the hope of embarrassing him in front of the man with glasses, but I never saw him with it after that, and wondered if he had thrown it away. Robinson was nothing if not canny, I realized.

Occasionally, I inspected the new contents of my wallet: the credit cards and receipts with phone numbers scribbled on, belonging to the man with glasses. I phoned these numbers to see who would answer, and, depending on the voice at the end of the line, I either hung up or said I knew the man with glasses and had they seen him or did they have his number because I'd lost it? One woman sounded friendlier than the rest. I called her a few times—with various excuses, such as not being sure I'd correctly taken down the number she had given me—before she got suspicious, and I spoilt things by hanging up in a hurry.

I started seeing the woman from Manette Street who had been going about with Robinson. 'Take her, old man. She's all yours,' he had said on one of the last nights I saw him. Robinson was always generous with things that weren't his to give. I took her nevertheless, but since Robinson had been there first my efforts were half-hearted and she quickly dropped me. I also sensed that she was still in touch with Robinson and that reports of my lack of prowess went back to him. I began to suspect that Robinson fed off self-destructiveness in others, that he had a talent for spotting weaknesses and enjoyed exploiting them.

I was sure that he could be malicious, as with the case of the locks to the office. It had still been easy to sleep there because I had not handed in my keys and nobody arrived much before ten in the morning. Then one night the locks were changed. Robinson's was the first name that came to mind. The condom boys would never have got around to changing locks without some sort of tip-off, and I could see Robinson telephoning anonymously and doing a nice little routine about me, saying he was looking for me because of money owing and he had heard that I was camping in the office.

Robinson went away without telling anyone. I stayed on, and life reached a sort of plateau, arrived at, I fancied, because some of Robinson's detachment had rubbed off. I became promiscuous. Since there was no point in imitating Robinson (whose personality consisted of countless imitations) I cast myself in a role that I could imagine playing. On the whole we stayed up too late and drank too much to be serious about anything, including sex. We were vain and caught up in shallow self-regard, perhaps understandably, because we were for the most part cleverer and more attractive than others, content to immerse ourselves. Most people practised sex for vaguely superstitious reasons. They thought if their sex life were all right then they were too. The more practical used it as a way to ward off insomnia.

I clumsily penetrated every woman I could manage as a way of reassuring myself that everything was fine, and once that was accomplished I developed the art of bed-crashing (spare bed preferable, if offered). There were surprisingly many willing subscribers and a night's sleep could often be had somewhere or other without charge or discharge. This boorishness fast became a standing joke around town, but those prepared to put me up, and put up with me, seemed privately grateful for not having to go through the motions before rolling over for the much more desired sleep.

There were still some bad moments before the wreckage of too many late nights finally overtook me, nights when, after a period of relative control, I needed to sense recklessness again. I was reminded of those wired-up dummies used in simulated car crashes: the gathering speed, the cruising way over the limit, faster and faster, until, no warning, BLOW-OUT: too late to stop, crash coming, spasm on impact.

'*Spasm on impact*,' I could hear Robinson saying, 'would be a great title for a film.' It would not, but I can't remember if I issued any challenge because the memory of Robinson uttering the phrase stopped me short. Because he couldn't have said it. Because I had only just thought of it, hadn't I? But in my mind I couldn't separate the phrase from the sound of his voice. Old man. I got nervous. I wondered how much more than the phrase—the metaphor perhaps if not the whole description—had been his too. Perhaps the white spaces had become so great that the only way to fill them was with some sort of fiction. Perhaps experiences I had imagined my own, which I had painfully reconstructed for myself out of the rubble of so many mornings after, were, in fact, quite simply plagiarized. I asked myself why, in a world regarded as essentially counterfeit, should one's own emotional worth be less fake than anything else.

I remember waking one last time in a fresh room, unfamiliar

IRISH
COFFEE

COCKTAILS

BAR
SNACKS

bed, strange place, no one around, a dark stain, not large, on the bottom sheet. The flat was dead quiet, apart from the ticking of an old-fashioned alarm clock, a Mickey Mouse alarm clock. I lay there unable to move, with a bad head and pressure on the kidneys. The silence of the flat got to me and I did not want to see what was in the other rooms. Apart from a few cut-up pictures I could remember nothing: not how or who or what. My eye felt swollen like it had been hit. Lying there, thinking about things, or, rather, trying not to think about things, I saw that I had dismantled my life so thoroughly that all that remained was a pile of cut-up gestures, like an unedited film sequence, bits missing. I was left in the position of playing voyeur to myself.

The flat stayed quiet and finally I overcame my funk. It turned out to be just an empty flat, of course, and I searched around a bit. Then I caught sight of myself in a mirror. The eye was starting to swell—what had happened? No idea, and the face that stared back at me from the mirror wouldn't tell. The flat seemed to be owned by a woman living by herself. Apart from dishes stacked in the sink, it was neat. The time was well after noon. The skyline outside failed to reveal where I was. Then the telephone rang. An answer-machine switched itself on. The name meant absolutely nothing, though I must have accompanied it home last night. The fact that she was nice enough to let me sleep in was the detail that worried me most. 'Careful,' I told myself, 'one of these days you'll wake up to blood on the walls.'

I went back to the suburbs.

I thought a lot about Robinson and tried to make sense of a new theory that he didn't actually exist. He was there, all right, a character, but all the little things about him—the lack of identification, the use of cash—suggested someone outside everything. Robinson was just there or not there, and this absence of a known past made him both as substantial and thin as a character in a movie. He was like a poster of his character. I see now that it was his ability to appear to operate entirely in the present that threw me, that in a sense made me try to obliterate my

Photo (preceding pages): Laurie Sparham (Network)

own past by these reckless excursions into white space.

When Robinson and I next saw each other I'd forgotten about my paranoia and thought I'd shaken off his influence. We met by chance in an after-hours bar where to get in it was necessary only to sign the members' book with enough of a flourish. He was sitting with a woman I knew by sight. He raised an eyebrow and smiled. I was with people so we exchanged little more than a brief hello. We were both drunk, of course, but he was well inside his limit and I was at the top of the slide. In his usual secretive way he suggested he was caught up in important work. I thought of the money roll in his back pocket.

His final gesture was to give me the wallet that I had taken from the man with glasses. The Harry Lime smile, the raised eyebrow. 'Old man? More use to you than me, I would have thought.' How much he knew I never knew.

I broke with the old places, made an effort to change, though this did not happen all at once. At nights I drove away from the centre, more often than not still drunk. I drank alone in suburban pubs and then headed north, always within the final boundaries of the city, driving at random until, exhausted and in the cusp of a hangover, I was in some strange place, perhaps a cul-de-sac in a modern estate.

In the pearl of early morning, I drove soberly and carefully back, merging with the first commuters, perhaps even passing for one. Moon on the wane high over the city, pale crescent in the lightening sky: on an elevated expressway a quick burst of speed and an illusion of skimming roof-tops, all undone by the slow choke of the Euston Road.

I quit drinking altogether, still staying away from the centre, and took to driving by night to Heathrow, cold nights with the window down and the radio on, out to Terminal Three. I treated the waiting lounges as my own. The nocturnal transit passengers sprawled on benches, all of them my friends and acquaintances, among whom I patrolled, a gracious host at the end of a party. Other times I waited in anticipation of a chance meeting with someone known—where are you going?—or with some stranger, selected by what process I could never decide. I was amiable, relaxed, fraudulent, my mind telescopic, cross-haired, seeking the pulse of blood, imagining its blossom. I saw myself in a crowd, taller than the rest, leaning forward with an unblinking gaze of curiosity.

LOUISE ERDRICH
OLD MAN
POTCHIKOO

Potchikoo

The Birth Of Potchikoo

You don't have to believe this, I'm not asking you to.

But Potchikoo claims that his father is the sun in heaven that shines down on us all.

There was once a very pretty Chippewa girl working in a field. She was digging potatoes for a farmer some place around Pembina when suddenly the wind blew her dress up around her face and wrapped her apron so tightly around her arms that she couldn't move. She lay helplessly in the dust with her potato sack, this poor girl, and as she lay there she felt the sun shining down very steadily upon her.

Then she felt something else. You know what. I don't have to say it. She cried out for her mother.

This girl's mother came running and untangled her daughter's clothes. When she freed the girl, she saw that there were tears in her daughter's eyes. Bit by bit, the mother coaxed out the story. After the girl told what had happened to her, the mother just shook her head sadly.

'I don't know what we can expect now,' she said.

Well, nine months passed and he was born looking just like a potato, with tough warty skin and a puckered round shape. All the ladies came to visit the girl and left saying things behind their hands.

'That's what she gets for playing loose in the potato fields,' they said.

But the girl didn't care what they said after a while, because she used to go and stand alone in a secret clearing in the woods and let the sun shine steadily upon her. Sometimes she took her little potato boy. She noticed when the sun shone on him he grew and became a little more human-looking.

One day the girl fell asleep in the sun with her potato boy next to her. The sun beat down so hard on him that he had an enormous spurt of growth. When the girl woke up, her son was fully grown.

He said goodbye to his mother then, and went out to see what was going on in the world.

Potchikoo Marries

After he had several adventures, the potato boy took the name Potchikoo and decided to try married life.

I'll just see what it's like for a while, he thought, and then I'll start wandering again.

How very inexperienced he was!

He took the train to Minneapolis to find a wife, and as soon as he got off he saw her. She was a beautiful Indian girl standing at the door to a little shop where they sold cigarettes and pipe tobacco. How proud she looked! How peaceful. She was so lovely that she made Potchikoo shy. He could hardly look at her.

Potchikoo walked into the store and bought some cigarettes. He lit one up and stuck it between the beautiful woman's lips. Then he stood next to her, still too shy to look at her, until he smelled smoke. He saw that she had somehow caught fire.

'Oh, I'll save you!' cried Potchikoo.

He grabbed his lady love and ran with her to the lake, which was, handily, across the street. He threw her in. At first he was afraid she would drown, but soon she floated to the surface and kept floating away from Potchikoo. This made him angry.

'Trying to run away already!' he shouted.

He leaped in to catch her. But he had forgotten that he couldn't swim. So Potchikoo had to hang on to his wooden sweetheart while she drifted slowly all the way across the lake. When they got to the other side of the lake, across from Minneapolis, they were in wilderness. As soon as the wooden girl touched the shore she became alive and jumped up and dragged Potchikoo out of the water.

'I'll teach you to shove a cigarette between my lips like that,' she said, beating him with her fists, which were still hard as wood. 'Now that you're my husband, you'll do things my way!'

That was how Potchikoo met and married Josette. He was married to her all his life. After she had made it clear what she expected of her husband, Josette made a little toboggan of cut saplings and tied him upon it. Then she decided she never wanted to see Minneapolis again. She wanted to live in the hills. That is why she dragged Potchikoo all the way back across Minnesota to the Turtle Mountains, where they spent all the years of their wedded bliss.

How Potchikoo Got Old

As a young man, Potchikoo sometimes embarrassed his wife by breaking wind during Holy Mass. It was for this reason that Josette whittled him a little plug out of ash wood and told him to put it in that place before he entered Saint Ann's church.

Potchikoo did as she asked, and even said a certain charm over the plug so that it would not be forced out, no matter what. Then the two of them entered the church to say their prayers.

That Sunday, Father Belcourt was giving a special sermon on the ascension of the Lord Christ to heaven. It happened in the twinkling of an eye, he said, with no warning, because Christ was more pure than air. How surprised everyone was to see, as Father Belcourt said this, the evil scoundrel Potchikoo rising from his pew!

His hands were folded, and his closed eyes and meek face wore a look of utter piety. He didn't even seem to realize he was rising, he prayed so hard.

Up and up he floated, still in the kneeling position, until he reached the dark blue vault of the church. He seemed to inflate, too, until he looked larger than life to the people. They were on the verge of believing it a miracle when all of a sudden it happened. Bang! Even with the charm, the little ash-wood plug could not contain the wind of Potchikoo. Out it popped, and Potchikoo went buzzing and sputtering around the church the way balloons do when children let go of the ends.

Holy Mass was cancelled for a week so the church could be aired, but to this day a faint scent still lingers and Potchikoo, sadly enough, was shrivelled by his sudden collapse and flight through the air. For when Josette picked him up to bring him home, she found that he was now wrinkled and dry like an old man.

Louise Erdrich

The Death of Potchikoo

Once there were three stones sitting in a patch of soft slough mud.
Each of these stones had the smooth round shape of a woman's
breast, but no one had ever noticed this—that is, not until Old Man
Potchikoo walked through the woods. He was the type who always
noticed this kind of thing. As soon as he saw the three stones,
Potchikoo sat down on a small bank of grass to enjoy what he saw.

He was not really much of a connoisseur, the old man. He just
knew what he liked when he saw it. The three stones were light
brown in colour, delicately veined, and so smooth that they almost
looked slippery. Old Man Potchikoo began to wonder if they really
were slippery, and then he thought of touching them.

They were in the middle of the soft slough mud, so the old man
took his boots and socks off. Then he thought of his wife Josette
and what she would say if he came home with mud on his clothes.
He took off his shirt and pants. He never wore any undershorts.
Wading towards those stones, he was as naked as them.

He had to kneel in the mud to touch the stones, and when he
did this he sank to his thighs. But oh, when he touched the stones,
he found that they were bigger than they looked from the shore and
so shiny, so slippery. His hands polished them, and polished them
some more, and before he knew it Potchikoo was making love to
the slough.

Years passed by. The Potchikoos got older and more frail.
One day, Josette went into town, and as he always did as
soon as she was out of sight, Potchikoo sat down on his
front steps to do nothing.

As he sat there, he saw three women walk very slowly out of
the woods. They came across the field and then walked slowly
towards him. As they drew near, Potchikoo saw that they were just
his kind of women. They were large, their hair was black and very
long, and because they wore low-cut blouses, he could see that
their breasts were beautiful—light brown, delicately veined, and
so smooth they looked slippery.

'We are your daughters,' they said, standing before him. 'We
are from the slough.'

248

A faint memory stirred in Potchikoo as he looked at their breasts, and he smiled.

'Oh my daughters,' he said to them. 'Yes, I remember you. Come sit on your daddy's lap and get acquainted.'

The daughters moved slowly towards Potchikoo. As he saw their skin up close, he marvelled at how fine it was, smooth as polished stone. The first daughter sank upon his knee and clasped her arms around him. She was so heavy the old man couldn't move. Then the others sank upon him, blocking away the sun with their massive bodies. The old man's head began to swim and yellow stars turned in his skull. He hardly knew it when all three daughters laid their heads dreamily against his chest. They were cold, and so heavy that his ribs snapped apart like little dry twigs.

Potchikoo's Life After Death

How They Don't Let Potchikoo Into Heaven

After Old Man Potchikoo died, the people had a funeral for his poor crushed body, and everyone felt sorry for the things they had said while he was alive. Josette went home and set some bread by the door for him to take on his journey to the next world. Then she began to can a box of plums she'd bought cheap, because they were overripe.

As she canned, she thought how it was. Now she'd have to give away these sweet plums since they had been her husband's favourites. She didn't like plums. Her tastes ran sour. Everything about her did. As she worked, she cried vinegar tears into the jars before she sealed them. People would later remark on her ingenuity. No one else on the reservation pickled plums.

Now, as night fell, Potchikoo got out of his body, and climbed up through the dirt. He took the frybread Josette had left in a towel, his provisions. He looked in the window, saw she was sleeping alone, and he was satisfied. Of course, since he could never hold himself back, he immediately ate the bread as he walked the long road, a mistake. Two days later, he was terribly hungry, and there was no end in sight. He came to the luscious berry he knew he shouldn't eat if he wanted to enter the heaven all the priests and nuns described. He took a little bite, and told himself he'd not touch the rest. But it tasted so good tears came in his eyes. It took a minute, hardly that, for him to stuff the whole berry by handfuls into his mouth.

He didn't know what would happen now, but the road was still there. He kept walking, but he'd become so fat from his greed that when he came to the log bridge, a test for good souls, he couldn't balance to cross it, fell in repeatedly, and went on cold and shivering. But he was dry again, and warmer, by the time he reached the pearly gates.

Saint Peter was standing there, dressed in a long brown robe, just as the nuns and priests had always said. He examined Potchikoo back and front for berry stains, but they had luckily washed away when Potchikoo fell off the bridge.

'What's your name?' Saint Peter asked.

Potchikoo told him, and then Saint Peter pulled a huge book out from his robe. As the saint's finger travelled down the lists, Potchikoo became frightened to think how many awful deeds would be recorded after his name. But as it happened, there was only one word there. The word *Indian*.

'Too bad,' Saint Peter said. 'You'll have to keep walking.'

Where Potchikoo Goes Next

So he kept on. As he walked, the road, which had been nicely paved and lit when it got near heaven, narrowed and dipped. Soon it was only gravel, then dirt, then mud, then just a path beaten in the grass. The land around it got poor too, dry and rocky. And when Potchikoo got to the entrance of the Indian heaven it was no gate of pearl, just a simple pasture-gate of weathered wood. There was no one standing there to guard it, either, so he went right in.

On the other side of the gate there were no tracks, so Potchikoo walked aimlessly. All along the way, there were choke-cherry bushes, not quite ripe. But Potchikoo was so hungry again that he raked them off the stems by the handful and gobbled them down, not even spitting out the pits.

Soon it was worse than hunger, the dreadful stomach aches he got, and every few steps poor Potchikoo had to relieve himself. On and on he went, day after day, eating berries to keep his strength up and staggering from the pain and shitting until he felt so weak and famished that he had to sit down. Some time went by, and then people came to sit around him. They got to talking. Someone built a fire, and soon they were roasting venison.

The taste of it made Potchikoo lonesome. Josette always fried her meat with onions.

'Well,' he said, standing up when he was full, 'it's time to go home now.'

The people didn't say goodbye though, just laughed. There were no markers in this land, nothing but extreme and gentle emptiness. It was made to be confusing. There were no landmarks, no look-outs. The wind was strong, and the bushes grew quickly, so that every path made was instantly obscured.

But not Potchikoo's path. At regular intervals new choke-cherry bushes had sprung up from the seeds that had passed through his body. So he had no trouble finding his way to the gate, out through it and back on to the road.

Potchikoo's Detour

Along the way back, he got curious and wondered what the hell for white people could be like.

As he passed the pearly gates, Saint Peter was busy checking in a busload of Mormons, and so he didn't even look up and see Potchikoo take the dark fork in the road.

Walking along, Potchikoo began to think twice about what he was doing. The air felt warm and humid, and he expected it to get worse, much worse. Soon the screams of the damned would ring out and the sky would turn pitch-black. But his curiosity was, as always, stronger than his fear. He kept walking until he came to what looked like a giant warehouse.

It was a warehouse, and it was hell.

There was a little sign above the metal door marked *Entrance, Hell*. Potchikoo got a thrill of terror in his stomach. He carefully laid his ear against the side of the building, expecting his blood to curdle. But all he heard was the sound of rustling pages. And so,

251

gathering his courage, he bent to the keyhole and looked in to see what it was the white race suffered.

He started back, shook his head, then bent to the keyhole again.

It was worse than flames.

They were all chained, hand and foot and even by the neck, to old Sears, Roebuck catalogues. Around and around the huge warehouse they dragged the heavy paper books, mumbling, collapsing from time to time to flip through the pages. Each person was bound to five or six, bent low beneath the weight. Potchikoo had always wondered where old Sears catalogues went, and now he knew the devil gathered them, that they were instruments of torment.

The words of the damned, thin and drained, rang in his ears all the way home.

Look at that wall unit. What about this here recliner? We could put up that home gym in the basement.

Potchikoo Greets Josette

On his journey through hell and heaven, Potchikoo had been a long time without sex. It was night when he finally got back home, and he could hardly wait to hold Josette in his arms. Therefore, after he had entered the house and crept up to her bed, the first words he uttered to his wife in greeting were, 'Let's Pitch Whoopee.'

Josette yelled and grabbed the swatter she kept next to her bed to kill mosquitoes in the dark. She began to lambast Potchikoo until she realized who it was, and that this was no awful dream.

Then they lay down in bed and had no more thoughts.

Afterwards, lying there happily, Potchikoo was surprised to find that he was still passionate. They began to make love again, and still again, and over and over. At first Josette returned as good as Potchikoo gave her, but after a while it seemed that the more he made love, the more need he felt, the more heat he gave off. He was unquenchable fire.

Finally, Josette fell asleep, and let him go on and on. He was so glad to be alive again that he could never remember, afterwards, how many times he had sex that night. Even he lost count. But when he woke up late the next day, Potchikoo felt a little strange, as though there was something missing. And sure enough, there was.

When Potchikoo looked under the covers, he found that his favourite part of himself was charred black, and thin as a burnt twig.

Potchikoo Restored

It was terrible to have burnt his pride and joy down to nothing. It was terrible to have to face the world, especially Josette, without it. Potchikoo put his pants on and sat in the shade to think. But not until Josette left for daily Mass and he was alone, did Potchikoo have a good idea.

He went inside and found a block of the paraffin wax that Josette used to seal her jars of plum pickles. He stirred the coals in Josette's stove and melted the wax in an old coffee can. Then he dipped in his penis. It hurt the first time, but after that not so much and then not at all. He kept dipping and dipping. It got back to the normal size, and he should have been pleased with that. But Potchikoo got grandiose ideas.

He kept dipping and dipping. He melted more wax, more and more, and kept dipping, until he was so large he could hardly stagger out the door. Luckily, the wheelbarrow was sitting in the path. He grabbed the handles and wheeled it before him into town.

There was only one road in the village then. Potchikoo went there with his wheelbarrow, calling for women. He crossed the village twice. Mothers came out in wonder, saw what was in the wheelbarrow, and whisked their daughters inside. Everybody was disgusted and scolding and indignant, except for one woman. She lived at the end of the road. Her door was always open, and she was large.

Even now, we can't use her name, this Mrs B. No man satisfied her. But that day Potchikoo wheeled his barrow in and then, for once, her door was shut.

Potchikoo and Mrs B went rolling through the house. The walls shuddered and people standing around outside thought the whole place might collapse. Potchikoo was shaken from side to side, powerfully, as if he were on a ride at the carnival. But eventually, of course, the heat of their union softened and wilted Potchikoo back to nothing. Mrs B was disgusted and threw him out back, into the weeds. From there he crept home to Josette, and on the crooked path he took to avoid others, he tried to think of new ways he might please her.

Potchikoo's Mean Twin

To his relief, nature returned manhood to Potchikoo in several weeks. But his troubles weren't over. One day, there was the police. They said Potchikoo had been seen stealing fence-posts down the road. But they found no stolen fence-posts on his property, so they did not arrest him.

More accusations were heard, none true.

Potchikoo threw rocks at a nun, howled like a dog and barked until she chased him off. He got drunk and tossed a pool cue out the window of the Stumble Inn. The pool cue hit the Tribal Chairman on the shoulder and caused a bruise. Potchikoo ran down the street laughing, flung off his clothes, ran naked through the trading store. He ripped antennas from twenty cars. He broke a portable radio that belonged to a widow, her only comfort. If a friendly dog came up to this bad Potchikoo, he lashed out with his foot. He screamed at children until tears came into their eyes, and then he knocked down the one road sign the government had seen fit to place on the reservation.

It was red, in the very middle of town, and it said STOP. People were naturally proud of the sign. So there was finally a decision to lock Potchikoo in jail. When the police came to get him, he went quite willingly because he was so confused.

But here's what happened.

While Potchikoo was locked up, under the eyes of the Tribal Sheriff, his mean twin went out and caused some mischief near the school by starting a grass-fire. So now the people knew the trouble wasn't caused by Old Man Potchikoo. And next time the bad twin was seen, Josette followed him. He ran very fast, until he reached the chain-link fence around the graveyard. Josette saw him jump over the fence and dodge among the stones. Then the twin got to the place where Potchikoo had been buried, lifted the ground like a lid, and wiggled under.

How Josette Takes Care Of It

So the trouble was that Potchikoo had left his body in the ground, empty, and something bad found a place to live.

The people said the only thing to do was to trap the mean twin and then get rid of him. But no one could agree on how to do it. People just talked and planned, no one acted. Finally Josette had to take the matter into her hands.

One day she made a big pot of stew and into it she put a bird. Into the roasted bird, she put a bit of blue plaster that had fallen off the Blessed Virgin's robe while Josette cleaned the altar. She took the stew and left the whole pot just outside the cemetery fence. From her hiding-place deep in a lilac bush, she saw the mean twin creep forth. He took the pot in his hands and gulped down every morsel, then munched the bird up bones and all. Stuffed full, he lay down to sleep. He snored. After a while, he woke and looked around himself, very quiet. That was when Josette came out of the bush.

'In the name of the Holy Mother of God!' she cried. 'Depart!'

So the thing stepped out of Potchikoo's old body, all hairless and smooth and wet and grey. But Josette had no pity. She pointed sternly at the dark stand of pines, where no one went, and slowly, with many a sigh and backward look, the thing walked over there.

Potchikoo's old body lay, crumpled like a worn suit of clothes, where the thing had stepped out. Right there, Josette made a fire, a little fire. When it was very hot, she threw in the empty skin and it crackled in the flames, shed sparks and was finally reduced to a crisp of ashes, which Josette brushed carefully into a little sack, and saved in her purse.

Notes on Contributors

Jeremy Harding is currently researching a television programme on boxing and the arts for the BBC *Omnibus* series. **John Gregory Dunne** lives in New York with his wife Joan Didion. He is the author of *True Confessions*, *Vegas* and *The Red, White and Blue*. His autobiographical novel *Harp* will be published next year by Granta Books. **Eugene Richards**'s previous contribution, 'Amazon' in *Granta* 16, is an account of the illness of his wife, Dorothea Lynch. His casualty-ward photographs are collected in *The Knife and Gun Club* to be published by Atlantic Monthly Press Books in the United States. **Edmund White** is the author of four novels. The latest is *The Beautiful Room is Empty*, a sequel to *A Boy's Own Story*. He lives in Paris. 'Letters to my Father, now Dead' is selected from the 'correspondence' between **Tomás** and **Teresa Pàmies**. **Mary McCarthy**'s books include *Memories of a Catholic Girlhood* and *The Group*. **Adam Mars-Jones** is a frequent contributor to *Granta*. His last piece, 'Remission', appeared in *Granta* 22. He is working on a long essay 'Masculinity and its Discontents' to be published later this year. *Given Ground*, **Roger Garfitt**'s next collection of poetry, will be published by Carcanet in September. He divides his time between Newcastle-on-Clun and Colombia. **Michael Ignatieff** is a Canadian writer and broadcaster based in London. His piece 'August In My Father's House' appeared in *Granta* 14, 'Autobiography'. Author of *The Russian Album*, he is currently working on a novel, *Real Time*, also set in the Soviet Union. **John Treherne** is a fellow of Downing College and director of a Zoology research group in Cambridge. He is the author of *The Galapagos Affair*, *The Mangrove Chronicle* and, most recently, *The Walk to Acorn Bridge*. **William Cooper**'s novels include *Scenes from Provincial Life* and *Scenes from Married Life*. He lives in London with his daughter. The East German **Rudolf Schäfer**'s photographs are in the Saatchi Collection. **Christopher Petit** directed the films *Radio On* and *Flight to Berlin*. He is currently working on a book about Soho. **Louise Erdrich**'s last novel was *Beet Queen*. Her story 'Knives' appeared in *Granta* 19, 'More Dirt'. She lives in Cornish, New Hampshire.